Southe Extraordinary History

Amazing True Stories from Southern Arizona Guide

"The entire Wild West didn't take place in Southern Arizona. It only seems that way because of the legendary cast of characters that roamed the landscape. That means a lot of great stories sprang from these deserts, grasslands, mountains and towns. What Jim Gressinger does so well is tell the stories behind the stories. He breathes life into this intriguing but often brutal history, connecting us to people and places in unexpected ways. The flavor of the times spills from the pages of this book in rich detail. Once you've finished, you'll be inspired to explore even more of this fascinating swath of country known as Southern Arizona."

– Roger Naylor
Travel Writer: Author of several books about Arizona and the American Southwest, including: Arizona Kicks on Route 66; Death Valley, Hottest Place On Earth; and Boots & Burgers: An Arizona Handbook for Hungry Hikers. http://www.rogernaylor.com

---

"A no-holds-barred look at some noteworthy Southern Arizona people and events."

– David Devine
Author of: Tucson: A History of the Old Pueblo from the 1854 Gadsden Purchase

Dedicated to:

My father, William F. (Bill) Gressinger, who
taught me to appreciate the lessons of history. He
was born in Tucson on Christmas Day 1919 and,
as of this 2016 printing, is alive and well.

ISBN: 978-0-9978680-0-5
ISBN: 978-0-9978680-1-2 (e-book)

Published by: Southern Arizona Guide, LLC

Cover and Book Design: Devil Dog Productions, LLC

Cover photograph: Southern Arizona Guide, LLC

Southern Arizona's Extraordinary History

Amazing True Stories from Southern Arizona Guide

Table of Contents

Southern Arizona's Extraordinary History

Introduction

This anthology is a collection of little-known, but amazing true short stories about Tucson and Southern Arizona from the archives of SouthernArizonaGuide.com.

Our Recommendations

Southern Arizona Guide is a content-rich website about our recommendations for the Best Dining, Lodging, & Things To See & Do. Included are our recommendations for Best Day Trips, Best Road Trips, Best Picnic Areas, Best Birding Hot Spots, and much, much more!

As of 2016, the Guide is 5-years-old and garners more than 400,000 annual visitors.

Since we launched in 2011, our 3 most viewed sections have been:

1. Recommended Things To Do With Kids (parents and grandparents love this section)

2. Recommended Dining, including our short Lists of the Best Mexican; Burgers; Pizzas; Sunday Brunches; & Steakhouses.

3. Local History, including Bisbee, Tombstone, Tucson and, and of course, the Apache Wars that raged throughout Southern Arizona in the 19th century.

Amazing, But Little Known Local Histories

It has been our pleasure to conduct the detailed research and write the local histories for a myriad of armchair historians of which there are hundreds of thousands. Presented in this little booklet are some of the most amazing true stories involving Tucson and Southern Arizona; an immense, unforgiving landscape and the pioneers who tried to bend it to their will.

Southern Arizona Guide Tours

Southern Arizona Guide Wine Tours Are Both Educational And Fun!

If you find these stories interesting, you might also enjoy our Guided Tours, including:

- Ghost Town Tours
- Wine Tasting Tours
- Tucson History & Libation Walking Tours
- Santa Cruz River Valley Tour

Descriptions of our regularly scheduled tours can be found at SouthernArizonaGuide.com > Guided Tours

We are also available for private charter tours for your family or organization.

Your constructive comments are always appreciated and personally replied to. Please email your comments to: Jim@ SouthernArizonaGuide.com.

A Fate Worse Than Death

How Tucson's Pennington Street Got Its Name

(a) Could it be named for some 19th century politician and merchant not unlike Estevan Ochoa, who established a successful business supplying Indian reservations and U.S. Army forts northeast of Tucson? He served as mayor (1875-76) and has a downtown street named in his honor.

Or (b) could Pennington Street be named for a prominent Tucson citizen, such as John F. Stone, superintendent of the Apache Mining Company for whom Stone Avenue is named, or Lt. Howard Cushing for whom Cushing Street is named. Both were killed by Apaches.

Or (c) None of the above.

Answer: (c). Pennington Street was named for a young woman and her pioneer family. Doesn't sound all that interesting, does it? However, you may reconsider after you've read the rest of the story.

****

What Does It Really Mean To Say Our Pioneers Were Rugged?

If we think of them at all, we tend to think fondly of our Arizona Territory pioneers. In the shallow backwaters of our imagination, we apply common descriptive terms to their exploits as they settled the West. They were rugged, determined, courageous. But what does that mean in reality?

Most of what we know about their ruggedness, determination, and courage comes from Hollywood movies. We are so often exposed only to general, sanitized, sensationalized, or romanticized versions of pioneering. Think of the 1940 Western, *Arizona*, starring Jean Arthur and William Holden. Old Tucson was created to make this popular movie and the set played the part of the real Tucson ca. 1860.

What do we actually know about the day-to-day lives of the first ranchers, miners, and merchants to arrive in Southern Arizona? So much of our history is the history of the men. But some of these pioneer men came with a wife and young children. What was it like for the womenfolk?

Arizona's Earliest Pioneer Women

If we try, we can imagine the daily hardship endured by our first pioneer women. They had nothing that today we would consider the essentials of life: no corner grocery store; no hospital; not even a Starbucks.

Sometimes we moderns like to romance "The Good Ol' Days". We think of them as a simpler time. And they were. Back in the Territorial Days, pioneers didn't have to deal with all the complex technology that has so engulfed our fast-paced lives and resulted in so much angst, depression, and stress.

They had no traffic congestion. Hell, they didn't even have automobiles. Often they didn't even have roads. No radio, no TV, no computer connected to the Internet with terabytes of data coming at them in a constant stream from every direction. Compared to us moderns, our Territorial pioneers lived in slow motion; hopelessly ignorant; pathetically primitive.

In the "Good Ol' Days, our earliest Arizona Territory pioneers had one simple question before them as they awoke every morning:

"How do I keep myself and my family alive one more day." That's about as simple as life gets.

This is the story of one pioneer woman who not only dealt with the incredible hardships, disappointments, and grief of daily pioneer life. On a day in March 1860, she came face to face with every pioneer's worst nightmare. This was the day that Larcena Pennington and Mercedes, her young student, were kidnapped by the Territory's alpha-predators, the Apaches.

Larcena Pennington

(Primary Source: Robert H. Forbes, author of The Penningtons: Pioneers of Early Arizona. 1919. Quotes in italics are from Mr. Forbes' book.)

Born in Tennessee, Larcena had seven sisters and four brothers. Soon after her mother died, her father, Elias Pennington, moved the family to Texas in 1857. Larcena was 19.

Crossing Texas was just a way to get to California where they hoped they would find prosperity. They had 3 wagons, one pulled by oxen, the others by mules, containing their worldly possessions, plus a small herd of cattle.

To get to California from Texas, they had to cross New Mexico. In order to cross New Mexico, they first had to cross the raging Pecos River. Many of their cows drowned. They lost the family Bible and most of the children's schoolbooks.

Arriving In Southern Arizona

In the months that it had taken to travel more than 1500 miles over incredibly harsh Southwestern topography, eight

1914 - The ruins of Fort Buchanan. Nothing remains today.

Penningtons, including the father, arrived in Southern Arizona, but had to stop at Fort Buchanan 3 miles southwest of present-day Sonoita. They and their cattle were exhausted. At least what was left of their cattle. The Apaches had stolen so many cows along the way, they barely had enough to call it a herd. Worse, Larcena was down with malaria. Malaria is incredibly debilitating, and often fatal. When the parasites enter the blood stream, usually from a mosquito bite, they destroy red blood cells by the billions. This leads to extremely high fever, massive headaches, severe joint and muscle pain, nausea, vomiting, and diarrhea. Victims become listless, unable to function. Coma and death is commonplace.

Even now, more than 150 years since Larcena contracted malaria, more than one million deaths and 300 - 500 million cases worldwide are reported annually. Back in Larcena's day, no one knew what caused malaria or how to treat it. If you lived, you were among the lucky few. Larcena was lucky. She survived.

Fort Buchanan To Tucson

For a while, the Pennington men contracted with the soldiers to supply the fort with vegetables and hay. The Pennington women sewed and mended uniforms. But at least they and their "herd" were now protected by the U.S. Army, such as it was.

When their contract was completed, the Pennington family continued west to the Santa Cruz River near Tucson where the river flowed perennially and fish were plentiful. While at Fort Buchanan, Larcena had met and fallen in love with a lumberjack named John Page.

They were the first couple of American citizens to be married in Tucson; then a dusty, stinky little town in the middle of nowhere comprised of a few hundred souls, mostly Mexicans and Papago Indians.

Canoa Ranch

Freight-hauling and logging were among the most important enterprises of that period. Larcena's siblings and her new husband were involved in both. And everything and everyone ALWAYS had to be protected from the Apaches. Only in the most desperate of circumstances would well-armed pioneer men venture out to hunt for game. The region was rich in wildlife: deer, antelope, bear, wild turkeys. There were even beaver in the San Pedro and Santa Cruz Rivers. But experience told them that they themselves would quickly become the hunted. A couple of lone hunters, be they Anglo or Mexican, were no match for the Apaches.

Not long after they were married, the happy couple was working at the Canoa Ranch just south of present-day Green Valley. Their employer had a sawmill in Madera Canyon, where John cut down pine trees that were milled in the canyon, then shipped by wagon to Tucson.

Larcena became a teacher for her employer's ward, an 11-year-old Mexican girl named Mercedes. When Larcena became quite ill, probably a malaria recurrence, John planned to move them out of the desert and into a cabin in the Madera Canyon forest near the lumber mill at the "Big

Madera Canyon Today

Rock". Today this is the site of the Madera Kubo Gift Shop. The hope was that the much higher altitude would help Larcena recover.

Madera Canyon

On March 15, 1860, John picked up his wife, her student, and her student's dog from the ranch in a wagon and headed up the canyon. Two miles below their destination at the "Big Rock" they stopped for the night and made camp among a pleasant grove of mesquite and oak trees beside Madera Creek. Five Pinal (aka Tonto) Apache warriors were watching from the surrounding hills.

Kidnapped

The next morning, John headed up the canyon to check on a load of lumber at the mill, leaving Larcena and Mercedes alone. Larcena was sitting on a rocking chair in her tent when she heard Mercedes' dog bark. Then she heard Mercedes scream.

Larcena grabbed her husband's revolver, but the Apaches

disarmed her before she could fire a shot ... a shot that, no doubt, would have brought John running back to camp.

The Apaches were armed with bows, arrows and lances, but no firearms. Four were young men, but the fifth was older and spoke a little Spanish. The older warrior told Mercedes that they had already killed John and that they would kill her and Larcena if they resisted. When Mercedes told Larcena that her husband was dead, she became hysterical and began to scream. One of the young warriors held a lance against Larcena's chest and threatened to kill her if she didn't shut up.

The Apaches stole whatever they could carry, including food and a feather bed. With their captives, the Indians headed northeast on foot. With Mercedes as interpreter, the older Apache told Larcena that this land belonged to the Apaches until the white man came.

(Don't let this attempt to engender sympathy for the Apache's plight mislead you. The Apaches had no friends among the many other Native American groups, including our local Tohono O'odham. All the other tribes hated the Apaches as much as the early American and Mexican pioneers.)

The Apaches were professional raiders, which is a polite way of saying they were highly competent thieves and murderers. They were also involved in the lucrative slave trade. As the very weak Larcena was being pushed and pulled up and down the rocky terrain, the older Apache, using Mercedes as interpreter, pointed to one of the younger men and told Larcena that he would be her new owner.

(If you were an early pioneer in the American Southwest, you probably would have done what most did ... demand that the U.S. Army exterminate the Apaches; which by the way was the official Mexican policy.)

As they walked, Larcena and Mercedes tore off pieces of

their clothes and bent twigs, and dragged their feet, so that their trail was easy to follow. At one point, one of the Apaches melted snow in his hands so that the captives could drink.

(Do not mistake this as a gesture of kindness. Their Apache captors knew the women needed to be hydrated in order to keep up.)

Presumably, the Apaches lied about having killed John to further terrify their female captives and give them a sense of utter hopelessness so that they would be easier to handle.

The Search Begins

Fairly soon, John returned to camp to find his wife and her student missing. He quickly understood Apaches were responsible. He gathered a few men from the mill and they began to follow the trail.

By sunset, the 5 Apaches and their 2 female captives had walked about 15 miles along the foothills of the Santa Rita Mountains east of present-day Green Valley and slightly east of what is now the ghost town of Helvetia. One of the Indians who was serving as rear guard ran up to the older, Spanish-speaking Apache and told him white men were approaching from behind.

Unnecessary Baggage

They started walking much faster, but Larcena could not keep up. Having walked all day and still weak from her illness, she could no longer hike up and down the steep rugged slopes. Eleven-year-old Mercedes was strong, but now Larcena was unnecessary baggage, and thus a threat to the Indians.

Arriving at the top of steep ridge, the Apaches made Larcena take off her corset and her skirt. As she turned to continue walking, one of the Apaches plunged his lance deep into her back. She fell over the side of the ridge, about seventeen feet. The Apaches followed her down the ridge, stabbing her repeatedly with their lances and throwing heavy rocks at her.

One of the rocks hit Larcena in the face rendering her unconscious. They dragged her body into a snow bank behind a tree, so as to not be visible from the trail, and then took her boots. Bleeding profusely from 16 vicious stab wounds and unconscious, the Apaches left her for dead.

Larcena gained consciousness a short time later and could hear her husband's voice coming from the trail. She tried to call to him, but was too weak to speak loud enough.

The pain from the deep stab wounds was excruciating. She fainted over and over, only to awaken each time to the same wretched misery. But at least she now knew John was alive and searching for her. It gave her hope; a reason to live, no matter what.

The Search Continues

Because one of the Apaches was now wearing Larcena's boots, John believed that his wife was still walking with her captors. He, and the other men from the mill, passed very near the ravine where Larcena lay more dead than alive. They followed the Apaches' trail for days all the way through the Rincon Mountains just east of Tucson and beyond the Santa Catalina Mountains that today mark the northern boundary of Metropolitan Tucson.

After a week of trying to follow the Apaches, John went to Tucson and recruited a posse. The search for Larcena and Mercedes continued.

Survival

After John had passed by Larcena, she fell unconscious again and remained in the snow bank for about three days before waking up in the middle of the night. She ate some snow and did what she could to deal with her grievous wounds.

Then Larcena went further down the ridge and fell asleep

Huerfano Butte

until sunrise. The next morning, she began looking around to figure out where she was. Knowing that Madera Canyon was to the south, she looked in that direction and could see a *"small sharp-pointed hill,"* almost assuredly Huerfano (orphan) Butte, about three miles west of what later became the mining town of Helvetia around 1891.

She remembered that she had seen the little hill as she and her captors headed northeast. She now had a way-point for orientation. Now she could find her way back to the camp in Madera Canyon ... if she survived long enough.

Extremely weak from her disease, hypothermia, and loss of blood; shoeless, and nearly naked; Larcena could barely stand. For the next several days she crawled the fifteen miles back to camp, surviving on *"seeds, herbage and wild onions, with snow water to drink."* According to Forbes; *"Night by night (unable to lie on her back because of her wounds) she crouched upon her knees and arms on the ground and dreamed of food; but when in her sleep she reached out for the pot of beans before her, she awoke to find her hands clutching only gravel."*

At one point Larcena spotted a rabbit grazing on grass that she desperately needed. In anger, she threw a rock and, almost miraculously, killed the rabbit. She ate it on the spot ... raw.

Once, Larcena came across a bear's den. She was exhausted and desperate to sleep there a while. Fortunately, she was sufficiently lucid to know that she didn't dare.

To avoid freezing during the cold nights, she would dig a hole in the dirt or sand with her hands. Then she would lay down in the depression and cover herself with the dirt or sand that she had scooped out.

Perhaps, we should add "resourceful" to our list of descriptive adjectives of Arizona Territory's earliest pioneers.

Map of the points of interest in the life of Larcena Pennington

Ten days after she was captured, and after many days crawling on her hands and knees, she made it to the top of a ridge. Looking down, she saw the road that leads to her camp and the sawmill in Madera Canyon.

Soon she heard the sound of voices and wagon wheels. She attached what remained of her badly torn petticoat to a stick to signal for help. She screamed. But the people in the wagon neither saw nor heard her.

It would be another two days of crawling and stumbling and staggering before she reached a recently vacated camp. The campfire was smoldering. Some coffee and flour was scattered on the ground.

With water from a nearby creek, Larcena prepared some

bread on the fire, made some coffee, and then rested by the warm fire for the night. Amazingly, alone in the wilderness and horribly disabled, Larcena had not become dinner for some passing bear, mountain lion, or pack of wolves. Any of these predators could have made an easy meal of her.

Saved ... Finally!

The next morning, March 31, 1860, Larcena followed the road up to the "Big Rock" and lumber mill. Forbes says that *"as she drew near she was seen, but not at first recognized. With clotted hair and gaping wounds, nearly naked, emaciated and sunburned, she was at first mistaken for an unfortunate outcast squaw and the men ran for their guns."*

This report understates her sunburn. All of her exposed skin was nearly black.

It was only after Larcena called out her name that she was recognized. But even then, one fellow insisted that she was a ghost because he couldn't believe that a 23-year-old woman could survive for two weeks under such incredibly difficult circumstances.

One of the men took Larcena into a building and had her fed and washed while another man went to get a doctor in Tucson and inform John, who was preparing for a third expedition to find his wife.

The first thing she asked for was a plug of chewing tobacco.

On April 2, Larcena was taken to Tucson where Dr. Hughes told some locals that he did not think she would survive. His assistant, Edward Radeleff, wrote down his thoughts upon seeing her condition.

"I saw the poor woman. Lance thrusts in both breasts and in numerous other places, bruised from rocks thrown at her by the Indians, almost everywhere covering her with blood, emaciated beyond description, her hands and knees and legs and arms a mass of raw flesh almost exposing the bones."

Despite the doctor's prognosis, Larcena recovered fully. The following December, while John tended to the care of his resilient wife, she became pregnant.

Almost as unbelievable, the young Mexican girl, Mercedes, was later found by the U.S. Army and traded for Apache prisoners at Fort Buchanan.

At this point, one might think that the poor woman had suffered enough. Surely Larcena and John Page and their children lived a long and happy life together, right? But in Southern Arizona during the early Territorial Period, happy endings were usually reserved for fairy tales.

****

When the Civil War began in 1861, most of the soldiers stationed in Arizona Territory to protect settlers from Apaches were ordered back east. This left the Anglo and Mexican miners, ranchers, and merchants extremely vulnerable to marauding Apaches.

In order to find work and some semblance of security, John, Larcena, and some of her brothers and sisters, moved to Patagonia where nearby mines at Mowry, Duquesne, Washington Camp, and Harshaw were productive. (SouthernArizonaGuide.com has some photos of this area, should you be interested.)

But in April, as he was taking a wagon load of supplies to Camp Grant northeast of Tucson, John was ambushed by Apaches. He was buried where he died: "at the top of the hill beyond Samaniego's ranch, on the old road; and all that Mrs. (Larcena) Page ever saw of him was his handkerchief, his purse and a lock of his hair."

In September, 1861, Larcena, now a widow, gave birth to a daughter, Mary Ann. Shortly thereafter, she and her siblings moved to Tubac, and later to a stone house along the Santa Cruz River, about a half-mile from the international border with Mexico. The area around their stone house was infested with Apaches, and at one point Larcena had to flee to Mowry, a small, fortified, mining town in the mountains a little southeast of Patagonia.

Tubac

Constantly moving in order to find the necessary combination of work and security, by April 1864, Larcena and her siblings were back in Tubac. By now, however, they were the only residents. All the other families had fled during the Apache attack of 1861.

Three years later, one of Larcena's sisters died of malaria. A year after that tragedy, in 1868, her brother, Jim, was killed by Apaches. In June 1869, her father and another brother were murdered by Apaches. The remaining members of the Pennington family then went to Tucson, and soon decided to move on to California, their original destination almost a decade earlier.

Their wagons were again loaded, but about twenty miles outside of Tucson, they had to return when Larcena's surviving sister, Ellen, became gravely ill with pneumonia. Despite the best medical attention available in Tucson she died.

Starting Over

Now there were only two Penningtons left: Larcena and her brother Jack. Jack moved back to Texas, but Larcena remained in Tucson. In August 1870, nine years after her first husband was killed by Apaches, she married William Fisher Scott, a Scottish lawyer and judge. Larcena and William had two children, a son and a daughter. Larcena refused to leave Southern Arizona, despite all the hardships, danger, and grief.

Larcena became a born-again Christian and one of the first members of the Congregational Church in Tucson, established in 1881. She was also named president of the Arizona Historical Society. Larcena lived just long enough to see the wild, lawless Arizona Territory, in which she and her

| Larcena Pennington is buried in Evergreen Cemetery in Tucson | Mercedes is buried at Holy Hope Cemetery in Tucson |

family had settled 53 years earlier, become the 48th state in the Union. She died the following year.

Larcena Pennington Page Scott (1837-1913) was laid to rest in the Evergreen Cemetery on Oracle Road in Tucson. She set a high standard for pioneer ruggedness, resourcefulness, determination, and courage.

Mercedes

After she was freed, 11-year-old Mercedes was returned to her mother in Tucson. Eight years later, she married Alexander Shibell, a successful deputy sheriff, merchant, and eventually, Pima County Recorder. They had 4 children.

Having survived the "fate worse than death" her future looked promising.

She died in 1875 at the age of 26. She is buried in Holy Hope Cemetery on Oracle in Tucson.

How Pennington Street Got Its Name

What is now Pennington Street was once called Calle de la Mission during the Spanish era because it led to Mission San

Cosme de Tucson on the west bank of the Santa Cruz River beneath Sentinel Peak ("A" Mountain).

Sometimes it was referred to as Calle del Arroyo that could be translated as "Ditch"; "Gully"; or "Ravine" Street because it was a shallow watercourse for runoff along the south wall of the old Presidio.

In 1871, the street was renamed to honor the pioneer Pennington family who once had a sawmill along this ravine. Larcena's second husband, William Fisher Scott, died a year after she was laid to rest. Scott Street, which abuts Pennington Street in Downtown Tucson, is named in his honor.

The Education of a Notorious Gambler & Gunman!

Sophie Walton was born a slave on a Georgia plantation in 1856. Her master was a Mr. Walton. In 1864, Mr. Walton could no longer keep his slaves. The Union Army had freed them and he could not afford to pay for their labor.

Sophie Walton

To his credit, Mr. Walton did his best to find jobs for his former slaves. But at this time Sophie was only 9-years-old, too young to hire out on her own. So he placed her in the home of a friend in Fayetteville, Georgia.

Mr. Walton's friend put her to work as a nanny for his children. In return, she received room & board, and a small stipend. However, now Sophie was separated from her family for the first time and she experienced considerable fear and loneliness. To her good fortune, Martha Fuller, the family cook, took Sophie under her wing and served as the young girl's role model and guardian angel.

Somehow, some way, Sophie had learned to play cards and, from all accounts, she was quite a good gambler. She could count cards and knew how to cheat without being detected, even by the grownups in her adopted family.

As her wards grew into young teenagers, she showed them how to play cards. Sometimes, their cousin, John Henry, would visit and he too enjoyed learning card games like poker and faro. From all accounts, he was a very attentive student.

Gambling was not John Henry's only education. His fam-

John Henry at 20

ily sent him to Valdosta Institute where he received a classical secondary (high school) education in rhetoric, grammar, math, history and languages, mainly Latin, but also French.

In 1870, when John Henry was 19, he chose to attend a dental school in Pennsylvania. By March 1872, he had met the requirements for Doctor of Dental Surgery, but his degree was withheld for 5 months until he reached age 21, as required by law.

Soon after beginning his dental practice, John Henry contracted what they then called consumption. We know this devastating disease as tuberculosis or TB. His mother had died from this disease when he was 15-years-old, as had his stepbrother the following year.

The doctors told John Henry that he had only a few months to live. Yet they gave him some hope that the warmer, dryer climate of the West might slow the deterioration of his health.

But John Henry persisted in dentistry, at least for a while. In 1873, he and his dental partner, Dr. John Seegar, won first place in the Dallas County Fair for *"Best Set of Teeth in Gold"; Best Vulcanized Rubber"; "Best Set of Artificial Teeth and Dental ware"*. Clearly the young dentist had talent and would have succeeded brilliantly in his chosen profession had it not been for his sometimes uncontrollable coughing while working on patients.

Over the next 7 years, John Henry moved West: Ft. Griffin, TX; Denver, Cheyenne, Deadwood and then Dodge City, KS, where he met U.S. Deputy Marshal Bat Masterson.

During this period, John Henry tried to practice dentistry, but as his disease progressed, he relied more on gambling to earn a living, the skills that Sophie had taught him.

He had also taken up with a Hungarian dancehall girl and sometimes prostitute, Mary Katharine Harony. Over many years, their relationship would be tumultuous, but she was the only woman with whom John Henry ever had a relationship.

These were tough towns comprised largely of hard men, many of whom had what today we call "anger management issues". Mostly they were armed young men overdosing on testosterone and alcohol. It was during this time that John Henry earned a reputation as a skilled gambler and a gunman to be feared.

In 1880, John Henry and Ms. Harony arrived at the next big thing; the silver-rich boomtown folks called Tombstone. It was here that John Henry reunited with a sometimes gambler, sometimes lawman named Wyatt Earp, whose brother Virgil Earp was U. S. Deputy Marshal for Arizona Territory and the Tombstone Chief of Police.

As lawmen, the Earps took a stand against lawlessness in general and an informal outlaw organization known as *The Cowboys* in particular. They were mostly stock rustlers and stagecoach robbers, but they also caused a lot of trouble while blowing off steam in the saloons and brothels of Tombstone. The two factions seemed destined to confront each other, which is what happened at 3:00 PM October 26, 1881.

U.S. Deputy Marshal Virgil Earp handed John Henry a sawed-off 10 gauge double barrel shot gun and, along with Wyatt and Morgan Earp, the four walked the two blocks past the rear entrance to the OK Corral on Fremont Street, there to disarm 5 Cowboys who were carrying weapons in violation of city ordinance. No one knows who fired the first shot.

They say that in 30 seconds 30 rounds were fired. When the dust and smoke settled, Virgil and Morgan Earp were wounded, Billy Clanton, and brothers Tom & Frank McLaury were dead or dying. Those who witnessed the most famous

John Henry
Holliday

gunfight in Old West history agreed. John Henry "Doc" Holliday had lived up to his deadly reputation.

In the months after Virgil was ambushed and maimed for life and Morgan was killed in Tombstone, Wyatt, Doc and several others loyal to the Earps went on a tear known as the Earp Vendetta Ride. They killed a lot of bad guys and then left Arizona Territory, never to return.

As a tubercular adult, Doc Holliday expected to die in a violent confrontation. He may have had a death wish, preferring instant death by gunshot to a languishing, pain-ridden and humiliating death by disease. In short, he expected to die with his boots on.

On November 8, 1887, at the age of 36, John Henry Holliday lay on his deathbed in a hotel near Glenwood Springs, Colorado. His nurse overheard his last words as he looked toward his bare feet and exclaimed, *"Now that's funny!"* One might wonder if, in those last days, he ever thought about the young former slave women, Sophie Walton, who had taught him the gambling trade that had given him a decent living in his latter years.

Wyatt Earp did not hear about his friend's death for two months. Mary Katharine Harony, aka Big Nose Kate, later claimed that she was with him to the end. She wasn't.

Today, you can belly-up to the same bar that served the Earps, Clantons, McLaurys, Mary Katharine Harony, and Dr. John Henry Holliday at Big Nose Kate's Saloon in Tombstone Arizona. We at Southern Arizona Guide consider it the best Cowboy Bar in America.

America's Longest War

From Left to right: Yahozha, Chappo, Fun, Geronimo

Which was America's longest war? In 2013, President Obama claimed that the war in Afghanistan is America's longest. But is that true?

First, let me say that "wars" no longer start with a formal "declaration of war" and seldom end with a formal signing of surrender documents or "peace accords". So part of the answer depends upon how we define "war".

Surely the U.S. was "involved" in Afghanistan shortly after the Soviet invasion of 1979; at least covertly. Thus, U.S. operatives have been involved in Afghan conflicts for 35 years. Yet we were not in a publicly acknowledged shooting war with the Afghan Taliban until October 2001 when we politely asked them to turn over Osama bin Laden and they refused.

That would make the Afghan War at that time, only 13-years-long. What about the Vietnam War? Clearly, the United States was "involved" in the Vietnamese Civil War when, in 1962, President Kennedy sent U.S. military advisors to assist the corrupt South Vietnamese regime against the vicious North Vietnam Communists.

The U.S. Vietnam War technically ended in 1971 when the U.S. and North Vietnamese signed the Paris Peace Accords. That would make the U.S. Vietnam War only 9-years-long. Even if one claims the Fall of Saigon in 1975 as the "real" end of America's "involvement", the Vietnam War lasted 13 years.

Both Afghanistan & Vietnam were long, hard-fought American wars for which the United States had little to show. But were they the longest? Thirteen years of bloody conflict is a "very long war". However, since it's founding with the ratifications of the U.S. Constitution and Bill of Rights in 1789, the United States was at war with Native Americans (aka American Indians) for almost 100 years. This was entirely a war of conquest.

True, the U.S. was not at constant war with all American Indian tribes for that entire time. But many of the "Indian Wars" were quite protracted. For example, the Sioux Wars lasted from 1865 to 1877 ... 12 years.

I think a strong case can be made for the claim that America's longest war was what we now term the "Apache Wars". It started with Cochise in 1861 and did not end until 1886. After 25 years of hostilities, almost the entire U.S. Army west of the Mississippi was essentially hunting one man ... Geronimo; "the worst Indian who ever lived".

Virtually all of the Chiricahua Apaches where transported by railroad from their homeland in Arizona to Saint Augustine and Pensacola Florida. The Chiricahuas would be held as prisoners-of-war for 27 years. Hundreds of these prisoners would die of malnutrition and disease.

The Bisbee Massacre

Brewery Gulch

On a cold December evening in 1883, five men robbed the Goldwater & Casteneda Store on Main Street that substituted for Bisbee's only bank. They did so believing that the mining company's payroll was locked inside the store's safe. What started as a quick and easy robbery ended in the death of almost a dozen people.

The robbers quickly discovered a problem. The mine's payroll had not yet arrived. Foolishly, the five robbers stuck around to steal what they could from the store, its owners, and customers. This took time. Time they did not have.

Two of the robbers stood guard outside the store, rifles

ready. Their presence attracted the attention of some of Bisbee's rough and ready citizens, who were typically well-armed at all times. Within minutes, four citizens lay dead or dying, including a New Mexico police officer who tried to intervene, and a pregnant woman, shot dead through a window by a stray bullet.

As the robbers rode south out of town, there was a hail of gunfire between them and the crowd of citizens that had gathered. Amazingly, none of the robbers was hit, except for a grazed jacket.

The Chase

One citizen jumped on his horse and headed north to Tombstone to notify the sheriff. He made the 22-mile trip in less than two hours and along the way passed the stage carrying the riches of the Copper Queen payroll.

The next day, Deputy Sheriff Daniels and his posse headed out to hunt down and capture the culprits. With them was a man who had just started a business in Bisbee – a fellow named John Heath. Once on the trail of the desperados, Mr. Heath did something that the deputy sheriff thought a bit odd. Mr. Heath tried to convince the posse that the robbers had actually headed north, perhaps toward Tombstone. Deputy Daniels didn't buy it.

Daniels and his posse continued the pursuit south and eastward toward the Chiricahua Mountains. Heath headed north. Eventually, Daniels tracked the robbers, found their exhausted horses and a rancher who said they had stolen five of his horses.

The posse continued tracking east, in the opposite direction of Tombstone, and came upon a prospector who had seen the robbers divvying up the stolen money and goods. And one more thing. The miner told the deputy that he had seen the robbers a week earlier getting instruction from their leader – John Heath. Daniels sent his posse back to Bisbee to arrest Mr. Heath and he, Daniels, continued to pursue the five robbers alone.

Capture

The Copper Queen Mining Company was not an outfit to be trifled with. They posted a reward and printed thousands of handbills describing the bandits and the articles they had stolen. They then went to the considerable expense of distributing these handbills throughout the Southwest and Northern Mexico. One robber was arrested in New Mexico when his barber recognized him from a handbill.

Two others rode to Eastern Arizona where one had a girlfriend. Unbeknownst to this fellow, his girlfriend had - in his absence - acquired a new lover. The robber gave his lady a gold watch, an item mentioned on the handbill, and her new lover recognized it and told Deputy Daniels, who then tracked down the two robbers and arrested them. One wore the coat that had been grazed by a bullet in the gunfight back in Bisbee.

That left two robbers who were not yet in custody. Daniels found them in Mexico, and with the cooperation of the Mexican authorities, brought them back to Tombstone to stand trial.

Verdict and Execution

Two months later, a jury found all five guilty of robbery and murder and sentenced them to hang. However, the jury – to the surprise of everyone – found leader John Heath guilty of only second-degree murder. The judge could do no more than sentence Heath to life in prison at the Yuma Territorial Prison (perhaps a fate worse than death).

Hanging of John Heath

Place where John Heath was hanged.

The honorable citizenry of Bisbee and Tombstone didn't think justice had been done. So they did what any civic-minded group would do. They formed a lynch mob and broke into the Tombstone jail to extricated Mr. Heath.

On Toughnut Street in Tombstone, Arizona Territory, the mob threw a rope over a telegraph pole. Mr. Heath tied a blindfold over his own eyes. His last wish was for the mob not to riddle his corpse with bullets as he hung from the pole. Tombstone photographer, C.S. Fly, duly recorded the event.

The coroner's report was interesting. It read in part: ". . . John Heath came to his death from imphysema of the lungs — a disease common in high altitudes — which might have been caused by strangulation, self-inflicted or otherwise."

On schedule -March 28, 1884 - the five robbers, Red Sample, Bill Delaney, Dan Kelly, Dan Dowd, and Tex Howard, were legally hung at the Cochise County Courthouse. They, along with Heath, were buried in Boothill Graveyard.

The Pioneer Hotel

The Fire That Destroyed Downtown Tucson

In the 1920's, one of Tucson's richest men was Albert Steinfeld. When he was 18-years-old, the German-born Steinfeld came to Tucson in 1872 via stagecoach to work for his uncle Louis' mercantile, Zeckendorf's. Originally, Zeckendorf's was a large one-story adobe building with a flat roof situated just west of Calle Real (in the Anglo-American era, it became Main Street, then Main Avenue), a dusty, often muddy, and always manure-rich transportation corridor running

Albert Steinfeld

north-south through Tucson that commenced in Mexico City and ended in Alta California.

So pleased with the efforts and business acumen of his young nephew, Louis made Albert a partner two years later and changed the name of their store to L. Zeckendorf & Company.

After a dozen years, Albert set out on his own. In the decades that followed, he acquired extensive mining & banking interests. But the core of Albert's business was in Downtown Tucson. The hugely successful Steinfeld's Department Store was located at Pennington and Stone Avenue where the unimaginative B of A high-rise is today.

The Year Tucson Got Its First Sky Scrapers

In 1929, when Albert was 75, he had long been president of Consolidated National Bank and the major stockholder. As such, he and son Harold were the force behind the building of Tucson's first "skyscraper", the 10-story Consolidated

Stone Avenue, Tucson, Arizona, showing Pioneer Hotel, Valley Bank in the Distance 309

The Pioneer Hotel in the foreground, and the Consolidated Bank in the distance.

National Bank building at Stone Avenue and Congress Street. This structure, now in service of Chase Bank, cost an incredible $1 million to build.

(Those who appreciate local history might find the huge murals on the mezzanine level of interest. But you have to check in with the security guard.)

Almost simultaneously, Albert and Harold built the Pioneer International Hotel, also on Stone Avenue a few blocks north of their bank building and cater-corner (or if you prefer "kitty-corner") to their Department Store. The 11-story hotel, became Tucson's tallest building. It was THE place to be and be seen Downtown. This beautifully designed "modern skyscraper" catered to the prominent and well-to-do, particularly of the growing business community. Tucson's largest Kiwanis and Rotary Clubs met here. The Cleveland Indians stayed here during Spring Training. It boasted the largest ballroom in the United States.

Designed by famous local architect Roy Place, the Spanish Revival hotel displayed beautifully ornate stone facades and an atrium. The hotel's promotional material assured guests that this elegant, thoroughly modern hotel was "fire proof".

Like its sister high-rise, the Consolidated National Bank building two blocks south on Stone, the Pioneer International Hotel cost about $1 million to build, back in the day when a million dollars was serious money.

The pool area of the Pioneed Hotel. It was a popular place.

A special newspaper section on the opening proclaimed the hotel *"A crowning achievement in the annals of Tucson's civic and commercial growth of the past decade and a harbinger of future unremitting progress."*

Everybody who was anybody enjoyed lunch in the hotel's Tap Room. Out-of-town shoppers, mostly from Phoenix and Sonora, flocked to the Pioneer because it was right across the street from Jacome's and Steinfeld's, Tucson's leading department stores. *(Jacome's (Hawk-ó-may's) was located where the Downtown library is today.)*

Over the years, many prominent Americans signed the Pioneer's guest register, including football great Knute Rockne, entertainer Liberace, former first lady Eleanor Roosevelt, Western movie star Tom Mix, President Lyndon Johnson, and cowboy philosopher Will Rogers.

When interviewed in 2000 by the Tucson Citizen, 94-year-old native Tucsonan, Roy P. Drachman said, "It was the best hotel in town for many years. The Pioneer used to have a roof garden, where in summertime they would have dances

The fire engulfed the upper floors.

and orchestras, with tables around the dance floor. This was in the '30s, right after liquor was [again] legalized. It was a popular place."

And it remained popular almost through 1970. By this time, Albert had been dead for 35 years. His son, Harold, was running the various Steinfeld enterprises, including Steinfeld's Department Store. Harold and is wife, Margaret, lived across the street in the hotel's penthouse on the 11th floor.

The Worst Day In Tucson History

Downtown Tucson was doing well until December 20, 1970. The Tucson Citizen Newspaper called it the *"Worst Day In Tucson History"*.

At 12:19 AM, emergency dispatchers took three calls: "fire at the Pioneer". Veteran firefighters initially thought these alerts were another of the many false alarms; until they saw the bright orange glow across the Downtown skyline.

Three minutes later, 3 fire engines and two ladder trucks arrived. They called for back-up ... lots of back-up. Fifteen minutes later, Tucson's entire fire fighting arsenal was battling the inferno: 11 engines; 4 ladders; 5 medical rescue trucks; 203 firemen.

When the alarm was first sounded, there were over 700 people in the hotel. Over 350 were attending the Hughes Aircraft Christmas Party in the huge ballroom. Of the total, most got out safely. Twenty-nine did not; including Harold and Margaret Steinfeld.

"Fire-Proof"? Hardly. The open stairwells acted as chimneys, spreading the fire quickly to the upper floors. The carpets and wallpaper, and Christmas decorations, burned like kindling.

Exacerbating the problem of rescuing those in the upper floors, the fire department did not have ladders tall enough to reach them. Consequently, some guests in the upper floors made "ropes" out of bed sheets and blankets and scrambled out the windows. A few made it to safety. Others in desperation threw mattresses out the windows hoping to land on them when they jumped. The sidewalks were littered with crushed bodies as if they had been ripe watermelons dropped from 100 feet in the air.

Many young children and elderly burned to death. However, most victims died of carbon monoxide poisoning. Harold and Margaret died of smoke inhalation. It was an unmitigated catastrophe.

Once-vibrant Downtown Tucson would not recover for more than 40 years. After the fire, major Downtown businesses, including its once flourishing department stores, moved to the suburbs. Downtown became a derelict. Once elegant buildings became vacant or housed dive bars & porno theaters. The social elite were replaced by the homeless, down & out alcoholics and/or drug addicts and prostitutes.

The Rest Of The Story

Some hotel guests, employees, and bystanders tried to

Louis Taylor at the time of the fire

extinguish the fire, while others helped firemen get the injured onto stretchers and out of the burning building. Among those was Louis Taylor, a 16-year-old Negro who had been hanging out near the Hughes party trying to score a few drinks.

In the aftermath, investigators determined that the fire started at two places on the fourth floor; clearly purposely ignited.

Tucson police soon arrested young Louis Taylor, accusing him of starting the fire as a diversion so he could steal from rooms and the Hughes party. Taylor maintained his innocence, but was convicted of 28 counts of first-degree murder in 1972 and sentenced to life in prison. Case closed ... at least for the next 42 years.

To the extent that there was something positive to gain from this tragedy, fire codes in Tucson and in cities throughout the United States were seriously upgraded. After the fire, any building over 4 stories tall had to have sprinklers and smoke detectors installed; as well as fire-resistant carpets, doored stairwells, etc. The cost of the retrofit was enormous. The cost of not retrofitting high-rises would have been even more expensive in lost human life and insurance claims.

To resolve another of the many oversights illuminated by the blaze, Tucson Fire Department immediately acquired the biggest ladder truck made at that time; 150 feet.

At the time of the Pioneer fire, their 100-foot ladders only reached the 8th floor windows.

The Curious Case of Young Louis Taylor

The fire prevention and fire fighting lessons learned on that horrible night were not forgotten. Young Louis Taylor was forgotten, at least by most folks.

At his 7-week trial in Phoenix, the fire investigator hired by the State of Arizona presented a profile suggesting that the arsonist was a young black man. Another investigator testified in Taylor's trial that an accelerant had been used in the fire. Yet that assertion was not supported by laboratory tests. Taylor, who is mixed Hispanic and African American, was convicted by an all-white jury during a time of racial tension in Tucson.

However, Judge Charles Hardy, who presided over Taylor's 1972 trial, publicly expressed skepticism about the jury's decision to convict the Tucson teenager.

For years after the trial, Judge Hardy maintained a correspondence with Taylor, sending him law books and Christmas packages.

In one letter he sent Taylor in the early 1980s, the judge, who died in December 2010, said he was negotiating with Arizona lawmakers to have the sentence commuted, but the deal was predicated on Taylor admitting guilt. Taylor refused.

In October 2012, attorneys with the Arizona Justice Project, a volunteer legal group that evaluates cases on behalf of inmates who claim they were wrongfully convicted, asked a court to dismiss the case or hold an evidentiary hearing.

The attorneys said several defense experts, using modern forensic fire science, would testify that they would not have ruled arson as the cause of the blaze. The defense team also alleged a prosecutor engaged in misconduct by not giving defense attorneys a laboratory report that said no "accelerants" were found and by talking to the judge without defense attorneys present.

More recently, an investigator with the Tucson Fire Department reviewed the available evidence in the case and was not able to determine what caused the blaze. Of course, many of the witnesses who testified at Taylor's trial were now

Louis Taylor a free man.

deceased and much of the original evidence had been lost or destroyed. So, forty years after the fact, arson investigators did not have access to all the evidence available to the original investigator, who still maintains that the fire was deliberately started ... by someone.

His attorneys tried to convince Taylor to plead "Nolo contendere" as the most likely means of getting out of prison quickly. Now, all Taylor had to do was plead "No contest" as a part of an agreement to set aside his original conviction and give him credit for time served.

At first, Taylor rejected the offer. Throughout his ordeal, he always maintained his innocence. However, he finally accepted.

In April 2013, Louis Taylor, age 59, was set free to start a new life.

Cochise

K.C., Ms. Karen & Neighbor Roy explore Council Rocks where General Howard made peace with Cochise in 1872.

Observations of the Few White-Eyes Who Met The Great Chiricahua Chief and Lived To Tell About It.

Unlike the many images we have of Geronimo today, no photograph or sketch of Cochise exists. We only know what he looked like from contemporary written accounts; mostly American and Mexican. These we owe to the very few people of European descent who lived to tell about their close encounter with the great Chiricahua Apache chief.

He was born about 1810 in the Chiricahua Mountains of present-day Arizona when the United States was a small, weak republic on the East Coast of North America; 2,000 miles and, given the transportation of the day, a galaxy away.

His life spanned the era of American expansion across

a huge continent that was then populated by hundreds of Native American tribes and millions of American Indians. For a decade, 1861 to 1871, Cochise fought the Anglo-American invaders of his homeland with everything he had. Between Pinos Altos in New Mexico and Tucson and Tubac in Southern Arizona, Cochise and his followers probably killed 5,000 Americans and Mexicans. During the same period, Cochise lost hundreds of men, women and children killed by Americans and Mexicans.

In 1874, he died in the Dragoon Mountains, located about an hour and a half east of Tucson at a place now called Cochise Stronghold. Ironically, in the end he was at peace with the United States.

Naiche

Many said that his youngest known son, Naiche, most closely resembled Cochise physically. But we also have written descriptions that tell us not only about his appearance but, more importantly, about his personality, his attitudes, and his extraordinary fighting and leadership skills.

Physical Appearance

Most record his height between 5'10" and 6'0". According to Lt. Joseph Sladen who, as aid to General Oliver Howard, spent 10 days in Cochise's camp in 1872, he "looked more than his height on account of his somewhat slender build, and his straight physique."

Captain Joseph Haskell was among General Howard's party during 1872 peace negotiations at Council Rocks in the Dragoon Mountains. Later he wrote:

"The reports that we have had of Cochise have always given us the understanding that he is old, used up, crippled from wounds and exposure, and of no account whatever as a leader or a chief. How mistaken we were. We met Cochise and 13 of his captains, and Cochise is as different from the others of his tribe, as far as we saw, as black is from white. When standing straight he is said to be exactly six feet tall. I took a good look at him and made up my mind that he was only five feet ten inches. He is powerful, exceedingly well built, bright, intelligent countenance, and as fine an Indian as I ever laid my eyes on."

At the time of the peace conference, Cochise would have been about 62; old age in the 19th century. At 5'10", he would have been 4 inches taller than the average Apache warrior.

Persona

General Oliver Howard

Of his persona, General Howard, who negotiated the 1872 peace agreement, wrote that Cochise's "countenance was pleasant, and made me feel how strange it is that such a man could be the notorious robber and cold-blooded murderer."

In the two years following the 1872 peace agreement, Cochise was a frequent customer of Al Williamson, a trader at Fort Bowie, who wrote, "Cochise never smiled. He was severe and grave of aspect."

Perhaps Cochise was not totally humorless. After he agreed to end his war on the Americans and settle down on the huge, newly-created Chiricahua Reservation, his warriors continued to raid across the International Border in Chihuahua and Sonora. Once when asked what his warriors were doing in Mexico, he answered euphemistically, "making a living."

Honesty

To his enemies, the Americans and Mexicans, Cochise was a thief. But unlike his enemies, he was not a lying thief. He told

Tom Jeffords

Tom Jeffords, his friend and only agent of the short-lived Chiricahua Reservation, "A man should never lie. If a man asks you or I a question we do not wish to answer, we could say, I don't want to talk about that."

Fred Hughes, who worked for agent Jeffords on the reservation, said of Cochise's peace accord with General Howard, "He kept his word till the day of his death." In Cochise's barbaric, merciless world, this was a very high standard for honesty.

A Surprising Discovery: Apaches Are Actually Human

In 1896, almost a quarter century after the fact, Sladen recalled his stay in the Chiricahua camp that resulted in his change of heart toward the Chiricahuas. It came as a surprise to him that the Apaches were actually human, like himself. He wrote that the Indians were "always cheerful, demonstratively happy, and talkative ... brim full of fun and joking, and ready to laugh heartily over the most trivial matters. They were especially fond of playing practical jokes of a harmless nature upon each other."

Fear And Respect

Among his own people, Cochise was sometimes as much feared as respected. Apaches would go out of their way to avoid incurring his wrath, particularly when he was drunk.

Sladen wrote that once he "heard screams from Cochise's wife and sister. I saw them fleeing in terror from his bivouac. He was striking and scolding them."

"It may have been during such a binge that his spunky younger wife twice bit him severely."

Fred Hughes wrote, "It was astonishing also to see what

power he had over this brutal tribe, for while they idolized him and also worshipped him, no man was ever held in greater fear, his glance being enough to squelch the more obstreperous Chiricahua of the tribe."

Another American recalled in a 1890's article, "A private soldier would as soon think of disobeying a direct order of the President as would a Chiricahua Apache a command of Cochise."

In the mid-1900's, Asa (Ace) Daklugie, son of Juh (pronounced Hó) told ethnographer Eve Ball that as a child he was warned not to even look at Cochise's wickiup because it might be considered disrespectful.

Power and Influence

Cochise was chief because his followers wanted and needed his leadership at a time when their world was being invaded and their very existence threatened. At the height of his power, late 1850's to mid-1860's, Cochise exercised almost absolute rule over several thousand Chiricahuas. He could bring together his own Chokonens and other bands to organize war parties of more than 400 well-armed, well-mounted, and well-led warriors. No other Apache chief; not Mangas Coloradas, not Victorio, not Juh, nor Nana nor Loco, had this much sway over so many Apaches. In the 1860's, Cochise's word was law to a people who largely controlled and raided over a 20,000 square mile area of the American Southwest and Northern Mexico.

All Apache chiefs were war leaders who were skilled in the art of raiding stock from the Americans and Mexicans; generous in sharing their loot with their people, and adroit in trading their excess booty for guns, ammunition, blankets, clothes, and whiskey.

Being a war leader required extraordinary close-combat fighting skills. Cochise was well-known for his skill with knife and lance. But Captain Cremony of the California Volunteers who fought Cochise at the Battle of Apache Pass, later wrote, "… no Apache warrior can draw an arrow to the head, and send it farther, with more ease than he." It should be noted here that most Apache warriors were more deadly with bow and arrow than a rifle; at least until they acquired the best modern repeating rifles in the 1870's.

Hatred

Cochise could be relentlessly bitter and unforgiving. In the 1860's, Cochise's hatred for the Mexicans was surpassed by his hatred of the Americans, who had needlessly hung several of his male relatives at Apache Pass. About the U.S. Army's treachery at Apache Pass in 1861, Cochise said, "I was at peace with the Whites, until they tried to kill me for what other Indians did; now I live and die at war with them."

Cruelty

His capacity for cruelty knew no bounds. Cochise could be lovingly compassionate and generous to his own people, particularly his relatives, but toward his enemies he showed no mercy. His captives were often tortured to death in the slowest, most painful, and humiliating ways. Captives brought alive to Chiricahua rancherias were usually given over to the women for torture. It was one of their specialties.

Revenge

When the Americans or Mexicans killed his people; whether in ambush, set battles, or the massacre of Apache women and children; Cochise retaliated with all the power at his command. In the 1860's, his Chiricahuas mostly warred for revenge against the Americans and Mexicans. Raiding for cattle, horses, mules and other useable items was still important for survival, but "an eye for an eye" became their primary motivation. In this sense, the Chiricahuas had a keen sense of Old Testament morality.

Flag over the ruins of Fort Bowie, a place frequented by Cochise after peace was established in 1872.

Leadership

Above all, Cochise was a superb leader. In battle, he led by example. Edwin Sweeney, who penned the most authoritative biography of Cochise wrote, *"Cochise did not establish political alliances like those conceived and molded by Mangas Coloradas, his father-in-law, who was the dominant Eastern Chiricahua leader for some twenty years before his death (or execution) at the hands of white soldiers in 1863. Nor did Cochise evince Victorio's skills in the art of guerrilla warfare. His fame was not based on a single whirlwind raid as was that of Nana, Victorio's lieutenant, and he did not possess the military genius of Juh. Yet each of these men was Cochise's ally at one time or another, and although they were not of the same band, each willingly fought under Cochise or at his side. All respected his leadership ability; his fierce, uncompromising hatred toward his legion of enemies; and above all, his courage in battle and his wisdom in counsel."*

Peace

Chief Naiche, youngest son of Cochise, and his war leader, Geronimo at Fort Bowie, September 1886.

By 1870, if the Americans and the Mexicans were going to stop the Apache raids that were slaughtering their citizens and ruining their economies, they knew they had to either kill Cochise or make peace with him.

In the end, the United States government at the highest level decided that it would be faster and cheaper to make peace: a peace they agreed to in October 1872, then completely violated only 4 years later in 1876.

The Chiricahua Apache's War with the United States during the late 1850's and all of the 1860's is called Cochise's War. Cochise died in 1874. During 1879 and '80, it was called Victorio's War. Then until 1886, the Chiricahua's war against the United States became known as Geronimo's War.

Following the 1876 closing of the Chiricahua Reservation, the raiding and killing on both sides of the International Border continued for another decade. In 1886, Geronimo surrendered for the fourth and final time. The once mighty Chiricahuas were never to return to their Southern Arizona homeland that Cochise had so ably defended against overwhelming forces, both American and Mexican. Today, ironically, more than 6,000 square miles of Cochise's former homeland in Southeastern Arizona is named in his honor: Cochise County.

Is Anyone Really Buried In Boothill Graveyard?

Are there really any bodies buried in Tombstone's Boothill Graveyard? Isn't Boothill just a tourist trap with fake headstones? Weren't all the bodies disinterred and moved to a new cemetery?

We've been asked these questions, or ones very similar, many times over the years. So often, in fact, that we were beginning to doubt that Boothill Graveyard is an authentic cemetery for the dearly departed in the Old West's most famous mining boomtown. So we decided to dig a little deeper, so to speak. Here's what we found.

Boothill *is* authentic. It was Tombstone's first City Cemetery, established in 1879. It wasn't called Boothill until the 1920's, probably as a result of Hollywood westerns or dime novels.

The Desire For A New City Cemetery

One of the more famous headstones on Boothill

After the new City Cemetery was established in 1884 at the end of Allen Street, what became known as Boothill was referred to as the Old Cemetery. Most Tombstoners wanted their loved ones buried in the New Cemetery, so there were few burials at Boothill after 1884.

In fact, after the New Cemetery was established, many locals had the bodies of their loved ones disinterred and moved to the New Cemetery. Presumably, they didn't feel comfortable with their deceased family members spending eternity next to thieves, murderers, rustlers, prostitutes, and Chinamen.

But Boothill is also a re-created cemetery. By the 1920's, Tombstone's boom years were long gone. Most residents had moved away and there was almost no one left to tend to the graves. Boothill became a garbage dump. Most of the early headstones were wooden crosses that had disintegrated due to the harsh elements, or had been stolen as souvenirs, or trampled by free-range cattle.

When John Clum, former editor of the Tombstone Epitaph as well as former Tombstone mayor, returned briefly to Tombstone in 1929, he went to the Old Cemetery to pay his respects to his wife, Mary. Some said he became distraught when he could not find her grave.

Soon thereafter, a few of the town's remaining citizens decided that the Old Cemetery should be cleaned up and put back together. They enlisted the Boy Scouts to clear the brush and debris. Old timers tried to recall where various individual's graves were located. No doubt sometimes memories failed.

On October 26, 1881, U.S. Deputy Marshal Virgil Earp, his deputized brothers, Wyatt and Morgan, and Doc Holliday killed cowboys Billy Clanton, Frank and Tom McLaury near the OK Corral. The large headstone in the foreground was obviously placed by cowboy sympathizers. It reads, "Murdered On The Streets of Tombstone". Judge Spicer ruled that the Earps and Holliday acted in the line of duty. However, the Judge's ruling did not end the killing.

Legendary Characters Are In Fact Buried At Boothill

Yet, there are many famous people buried in Boothill Grave-yard for which there is reasonable certainty as to the location of their grave. For example, China Mary was buried at Boothill in 1906. She was the undisputed ruler of Hoptown, the Chinese neighborhood in Tombstone. Her tombstone is the actual site of her grave. Dutch Annie, "Queen of the Red Light District", is buried where her marker rests. She was a popular madam and gave generously to many worth causes and men down on their luck.

Billy Clanton, Tom & Frank McLaury are buried where their headstones indicate. John Heath was the mastermind of the robbery that resulted in the Bisbee Massacre. He was lynched by a mob in 1884. His 5 accomplices were legally

John Heath of Bisbee Massacre fame is buried here.

hanged that same year. All of their gravesites are reasonably certain.

Their final resting place, and many others, are known because their funerals were major events attended by hundreds, sometimes thousands of mourners & gawkers.

Yet the precise gravesites of many will never be known because either: (a) no one knew them at the time they were buried, or (b) friends & family moved away and their tombstones were lost to time and neglect. That's why you see so many "Unknown" grave markers at Boothill.

Locating The Graves Today

The tombstones in Boothill Graveyard are relatively new, replacing ones that withered away or were stolen. Visitors to Boothill can purchase a booklet with the names & locations of about 250 graves out of the 300+ graves that are actually there.

Texas John Slaughter

Slaughter Ranch Museum

Arizona's Meanest Little Good Guy!

By Roger Naylor

(At SouthernArizonaGuide.com we occasionally invite others to share their extraordinary stories, art, photographs, and videos with our visitors. Roger Naylor is a talented travel writer who writes about Arizona most notably in Arizona Republic and Arizona Highways. He has authored many books, including: Boots & Burgers: An Arizona Handbook for Hungry Hikers and Arizona Kicks on Route 66. *Visit his website at: http://www.rogernaylor.com.*

Roger has granted us permission to reprint his telling of Texas John Slaughter's life at Rancho San Bernardino; now a fine museum adjacent to a wildlife refuge.)

This is a great porch. The shady veranda stretches along the entire front of the house. Views extend across green

John Slaughter

pastures streaked with wildflowers into the rolling hills of Mexico. It's a comfortable porch. It's the kind of place where you want to settle in after dinner and enjoy a quiet hour or two as the evening cools.

John Slaughter, who was a Confederate soldier, Texas Ranger and Cochise County sheriff, loved this porch. He was sitting there one day with his family when a cloud of dust swirled up from the south. Pancho Villa and his army rode onto Slaughter's ranch. After a forced march, the famished soldiers began killing and butchering cattle.

Slaughter, in his 70s, pushed up out of his chair, strapped on his gun and ordered his horse saddled. He rode alone through the long grass meadow, across the border to confront Villa and his men. He was gone for a while but when he returned, he carried a sack of 20-dollar gold pieces. Even near the end of his days, Texas John Slaughter was not a man to be trifled with.

Fifteen miles east of Douglas, Slaughter Ranch is a little-known treasure of Cochise County. Its 300 acres are the remains of a cattle empire that once spanned more than 100,000 acres. The property is now a living museum. Everything has been restored to a late-19th-century appearance. The adobe ranch house has been carefully refurbished, as have numerous outbuildings. A white picket fence frames the wide lawn, gnarled trees drape the spring-fed pond and livestock graze the meadows.

'Meanest Good Guy'

I'm standing on that same porch, gazing across the pasture

into Mexico. It has been a spectacular monsoon season in this corner of the state, and everything is lush and green. As I admire the verdant oasis, I think about the old man swinging onto the saddle, no doubt stiffened by age, probably more perturbed at having to give up his porch chair than fearful of facing down a large number of armed men. For the former lawman, it was nothing new. Slaughter is one of those larger-than-life Western figures who have slipped through the cracks of history.

John Horton Slaughter was born in Louisiana in 1841 but soon moved to Texas. As a young man, he joined the Texas Rangers and later fought for the Confederacy during the Civil War. He raised cattle and was one of the first to drive herds over the Chisholm Trail. Slaughter stood just 5 feet, 6 inches tall and was prone to stuttering. But there was something about his penetrating dark eyes that warned people against taking him lightly.

Slaughter moved from Texas to Arizona in the late 1870s. His first wife died of smallpox before completing the trip. Slaughter met and married young Viola Howell soon afterward. At first, her parents disapproved because of the couple's age difference — he was 38, she was 17 — but eventually consented and even lived with them at the ranch.

The Slaughters first settled south of Tombstone. This was during the mining boom, when men named Earp and Clanton walked the streets. In 1886, just five years after the Gunfight at the O.K. Corral, Slaughter was elected Cochise County sheriff.

He wore a pearl-handled .44 and carried a 10-gauge shotgun. His method of keeping the peace was simple. He politely warned ne'er-do-wells to leave town. They didn't get a second warning. He proved fearless in any kind of shootout and relentless when tracking outlaws. He never returned without a prisoner or, more often than not, the remains of a prisoner. One writer referred

to Slaughter as "the meanest good guy who ever lived." Historians credit Slaughter more than anyone else with cleaning up the Arizona Territory.

Place of Tranquility

After serving two two-year terms, the lawman retired to his ranch. Slaughter had bought the great swath of land in 1884. The original Mexican land grant of 73,240 acres was sold in 1822 to Ignacio Perez. But Apaches drove him from his home just a few years later. Slaughter purchased the grant from the heirs of Perez, also buying up adjacent property to establish one of the most successful cattle ranches in the region.

Slaughter Ranch is now a National Historic Landmark. The ranch manager welcomes guests and offers tours of the buildings. In addition to the sprawling home are a granary, commissary, wash house, ice house and car shed. Each structure is a mini-museum, stocked with original and period furnishings and equipment.

Every room offers a new lesson about life on the frontier. Because town was far away, the Slaughters sold dry goods out of the commissary. Beef, vegetables and dairy products were preserved in the stone ice house. Ice blocks weighing 300 pounds were wrapped in sawdust and burlap and hauled by wagon from Douglas. The built-in china cabinet and fancy windows were ordered through the Sears, Roebuck & Co. catalog. The single men working on the ranch ate standing up in the cowboy dining room.

Slaughter was fascinated by technology and had the first telephone in the territory. He also had six automobiles, although he never learned to drive.

As much as I love the history of the place, I spend most of my visit outside, drawn by the beautiful grounds and chorus of birdsong. The 1-acre pond is ringed by shade trees and populated by ducks and herons. A vermillion flycatcher flashes past me in a streak of vivid red. Hummingbirds buzz like bees. As I walk near the water, croaking bullfrogs leap from the bank by the bucketful. Benches and picnic tables are scattered about. I take advantage of most of them.

Atop the mesa east of the pond, ruins of an old fort can be seen. During the Mexican Revolution, the U.S. Army established a series of outposts along the border, including this one that was garrisoned until 1923. Pathways lead through the stone rubble and present extensive views of mountains and Mexico.

Wildlife Refuge

The trails from the outpost continue onto the adjoining San Bernardino National Wildlife Refuge. The 2,369-acre refuge was established in 1982 to protect what remained of precious wetlands at the headwaters of the Rio Yaqui. This large marsh serves as a migration route for a variety of wildlife, including birds winging their way from the tropics.

In 2009, a rare blue mockingbird was spotted at Slaughter Ranch, only the fifth sighting in the United States. The event lured birders by the thousands to the far-flung oasis. Between San Bernardino and nearby Leslie Canyon National Wildlife Refuge, at least 335 bird species have been recorded. The wetland habitats also support such threatened species as Yaqui catfish, chub and topminnow. The only remaining population of San Bernardino springsnails in the United States exists at the ranch.

I follow the trails into the refuge for a bit, but I don't have time to go far. Besides, a bench by the pond is calling me.

Slaughter died in 1922. He is buried in Douglas. Yet I wouldn't be surprised if, on an evening, just past supper-time, the porch swing begins to creak as if someone just settled in and got comfortable.

Miracle On An Orphan Train To Arizona

Sometime in 1904, 40 Irish orphans boarded an orphan train headed for Arizona. Why? Allow me to explain.

In late 19th & early 20th century New York, newly arrived Irish Catholics were considered low-class by other ethnically "Anglo-Saxon" groups, such as German, English, & Dutch, who were mostly Protestant.

The Irish

"Low-class" is perhaps too mild a term. The Irish were considered hardly better than Negroes, whom most Anglos believed were sub-human. Odd as it may seem to us today, the fair-skinned, blonde or red-headed Irish were not considered white in a time and place that white supremacy was a given.

Consequently, migrants from the Emerald Isle faced horrific discrimination. "Irish need not apply" was a common sign in the windows of many Eastern businesses. The Irish in New York City languished in hopeless poverty, where they had inferior housing, food, medical treatment, and education (if at all); and where hope for a better future was almost non-existent.

Moreover, there seemed to be no end to the number of Irish street urchins. The orphanages run by Catholic nuns could not accommodate them all. Public records show that about 150 Irish children were abandoned every month and there were not nearly enough adoptive homes in the area to save them from a hellish life on New York City streets.

The Mexicans

At the same time, out west in Arizona, the Anglo pioneers accepted the Irish as just another group of Western European descent. In other words, in the West, the Irish were considered white. Mexicans, however, were another matter.

Like the Irish, most Mexicans were Roman Catholic. Yet Mexicans, most of whom were low-wage laborers in the fields or mines, were treated as badly by the dominant Anglo communities as were the Irish in New York. Mexican workers were often physically abused by their Anglo employers and cheated out of hard-earned pay.

In the American Southwest in the late 19th & early 20th century, most Mexican-American children grew up in shacks with dirt floors; where water was too scarce for bathing; where they received inferior food, medical treatment, and education (if at all); and where hope for a better future was almost non-existent.

These distinctions of race and religion were seldom more apparent than in October 1904 in the bustling copper mining communities of Clifton & Morenci' in Southeastern Arizona.

Weeks earlier, three Catholic nuns and four nurses from the New York Foundling Hospital along with 40 Irish orphans boarded an "orphan" train headed for Arizona. There,

according to plan, these children would be adopted by good Catholic families and grow up with opportunity in a labor-starved region of the American West. For these nuns, the primary, and perhaps only, criterion for adoption was that the new families had to be good Catholics.

In Southeastern Arizona, Catholic meant Mexican, and Mexican meant inferior. From the perspective of the Arizona white population, Mexicans were down there with other people of color: Negroes, Chinese, and American Indians. Of course, in a pre-politically correct era, whites would have used common pejorative terms for these they considered inferior. Such were the racial attitudes in Clifton and Morenci' when the New York nuns, nurses, and orphans arrived at the Clifton Catholic Church on October 1, 1904.

The Miracle

What the nuns apparently did not realize was that the long, hot, arduous train ride across this vast United States had miraculously transformed their despised Irish charges into superior "white" children.

They proceeded according to plan and 16 pale, blond, primly-dressed children were given to various Mexican families that had been chosen by the local priest. Afterward, the nuns took the remaining orphans 4 miles up to Morenci' and repeated the simple adoption process until all the Irish orphans had homes with good Catholic families.

The Mob

The dominant Anglo communities of Clifton and Morenci' were incensed. To them, the very idea of placing white children with Mexican families was nothing less than child abuse. The nuns were vilified as "white-slavers selling children to drunken-whore savages."

First, an armed white mob formed in Morenci' where it threatened to lynch the priest and nuns if they didn't retrieve the Irish children and hand them over to white families.

Then a similar mob gathered in Clifton armed with buckets of tar and feathers, a rope and gasoline. Here they "persuaded" a local posse to kidnap the orphans from their new Mexican families.

One white woman who led the revolt said, "They (Mexican women) all had dirty faces, and wore black shawls over them, and they had ragged dresses on." Another white women said, "...most of the Mexicans are unwashed and infested with vermin."

One of the New York sisters later wrote. "(white) Women called us vile names, and some of them put pistols to our heads. They said there was no law in that town; that they made their own laws. We were told to get the children from the Spaniards (meaning the Mexicans). If we did not we would be killed."

No criminal charges were ever brought, but the matter ended up in civil court. The trial judge sanctioned the "vigilante justice" and awarded the orphans to the Anglos who had kidnapped them. No Mexicans were allowed to testify.

An appeals court agreed with the lower court and approved the placement of the orphans with "the good women of the place." The U.S. Supreme Court ruled that it lacked jurisdiction.

Chiricahua Apache Warrior Women

Lozen & Dahteste

In the late 1870's, to engineer the official Indian policy of "concentration", the United States government forced Victorio and his band of Warm Springs Chiricahua Apaches to move from the land they held sacred in New Mexico to the dreaded San Carlos Reservation about 35 miles east of Globe, AZ and 140 miles north of Tucson.

At San Carlos, Chiricahua Apache survival was nearly impossible. So, in 1877, Victorio and 310 of his followers, men, women and children, escaped the reservation. To survive they had only one choice ... to raid. They stole cattle, horses, guns, ammunition and whatever else they needed.

The stories of the Chiricahua Apache's fight to keep their

homeland and way of life has been told many times, mostly by White-Eyes and Mexicans, and usually in the most self-serving manner. However, fairly recently the outside world learned that among the hostile Chiricahuas participating fully in battle after battle beside their male counterparts were a couple of extraordinary women fighters.

For two generations after the end of the Apache Wars, the Chiricahuas were very reluctant to tell their American over-seers about their warrior women for fear that the ignorant, bigoted, judgmental White-Eyes would think these Apache women indecent or impure for living un-chaperoned among unrelated men while on the warpath. White-Eyes had no idea that Apache sexual standards put Victorian morals to shame.

It would be well into the 20th century before the non-Apache world would hear about these two amazing women.

Charlie Smith, named so by White soldiers because his Apache name they could not pronounce, was interviewed by Eve Ball who asked why Chiricahuas are so reluctant to speak about Lozen, known to Apaches as *The Warrior Woman*. Mr. Smith told the author, "When actually on the warpath the Apaches were under very strict rules. Even words for common things were different. Women could go with their husbands, but they could not live together. No unmarried women were permitted. Lozen? No, she was not married; she never married. But to us she was as a Holy Woman and she was regarded and treated as one. White Painted Woman *(an Apache deity)* herself was not more respected. And she was brave. Geronimo sent her on missions to the military officers to arrange for meetings with him, or to carry messages."

Lozen (ca. 1840 – 1890)

Among her people Lozen is legend. She was the younger sister of the great chief of the Warm Springs Chiracahua Apaches, Victorio, who told his followers "Lozen is my right hand ... strong as a man, braver than most, and cunning in strategy. Lozen is a shield to her people."

She was a ferocious warrior and perceptive seer. She fought along side her brother and his followers as they attacked, and were attacked, by Americans who, with the advantage of vastly superior numbers and technology, had stolen the Apache's ancestral homelands in southwestern New Mexico.

Lozen

James Kaywaykla was a young Apache lad at this time. Many decades later, he told this story to Eve Ball who published it in her authoritative 1970 book entitled, *In The Days Of Victorio: Reflections of a Warm Springs Apache.*

Crossing The Rio Grande To Safety

Fleeing the U.S. Army, Lozen led a group of mounted Apache women and children to the raging Rio Grande into Mexico. Seated behind his grandmother on a horse as the group approached the fast-moving river, Kaywaykla knew that his grandmother and the other women were terrified of drowning. They were too frightened to cross the river. But if they didn't, they would be either captured or killed by the pursuing Americans.

Then, says Kaywayla, "I saw a magnificent woman on a beautiful horse—Lozen, sister of Victorio."

"High above her head she held her rifle. There was a glitter as her right foot lifted and struck the shoulder of her horse. He reared, then plunged into the torrent. She turned his head upstream, and he began swimming."

Immediately, the other women and children followed her into the current. Amazingly, they all reach the far bank of the river, cold and wet but alive. Once across, Lozen rode up to Kaywaykla's grandmother and said, "You take charge, now. I must return to the warriors."

At this point, Victorio's warriors were fighting to stay between their women, children, and elderly, and the advancing U.S. cavalry. Lozen drove her horse back across the wild river and returned to fight the Americans.

Note: to understand these circumstances, you need to know at least two things. First, the Apache warriors were almost always at a disadvantage when fighting the Americans and Mexicans because they had their families with them. Imagine any military outfit doing battle while shielding their aged parents, their young children, and their pregnant women. And still, the Chiricahua Apache, out-fought the armies of two "modern" nations with the proverbial one hand tied behind their backs.

Second, these Apache women warriors could slit your throat at close range or blow your brains out with a rifle bullet at a hundred yards as well as any man. Not to mention that their endurance was way too much for the pursuing armies, a fact often acknowledged by famed Indian fighter, General George Crook. "No White soldier can catch an Apache who doesn't want to be caught."

According to Kaywaykla, "She could ride, shoot, and fight like a man, and I think she had more ability in planning military strategy than did Victorio." He also remembers Victorio saying, *"I depend upon Lozen as I do Nana"*, Victorio's uncle and patriarch of the band.

Kaywaykla and other Chiricahuas also commented on her remarkable horsemanship. "No man in the tribe was more skillful in stealing horses or stampeding a herd than she." But Lozen was also well-known for her extraordinary ability to tame wild horses and to care for them. She was particularly adroit at treating the hooves and legs of lame horses. That was just one of her "Powers".

Note: now you need to know a third thing. Almost all Apaches have "Power". An Apache's Power is granted by Ussen, the Apache God of Creation. Some had the Power to divine the future; others the Power to heal; still others the Power to locate food. Chief Nana had the extraordinary Power to locate ammunition. Geronimo had the Power to heal. Moreover, his capacity for clairvoyance was legendary among his people. For this, the Chiricahuas both revered and feared him.

Stealth And Cunning

In late 1880, Lozen leaves her band to escort a young mother and her newborn across the brutally harsh Chihauhua Desert in northern Mexico to the Mescalero Apache Reservation in western New Mexico to spare them the horrific hardships faced by their band as they fled before the well-equipped armies of Mexico and the United States.

Beginning the perilous journey on foot with only a rifle, a cartridge belt, a knife, and a meager three-day supply of food, she had to evade the American and Mexican cavalry as well as Anglo and Mexican settlers and their (usually drunken) militias.

In a few days, they needed more food, but she was afraid to use her rifle to hunt because a gunshot would betray their presence. Ever resourceful, she uses her knife to kill and butcher a stray longhorn. *(Do you have any idea how difficult that would be? It's not like you can just walk up to a longhorn and slit its throat.*

Soon thereafter she steals a Mexican cavalry horse for the new mother, barely escaping through a volley of gunfire.

Employing all her strength and cunning, she then steals a Mexican cowboy's horse for herself and disappears before he can give chase. A few days later she steals a soldier's saddle, rifle, ammunition, blanket, and canteen. After weeks of trudging, riding, and stealing their way through the most dangerous region for any Apache, she delivers the mother and baby safely to the Mescalero reservation in present-day New Mexico.

It was there that she learns that Mexican soldiers and their Tarahumara scouts had ambushed Victorio and his band at Tres Castillos in northeastern Chihuahua.

The Mexican Destruction of Victorio

On October 14th, the Mexican Commander Terrazas and his battle-hardened troops, surprised Victorio's Apaches, and in the boulders of Tres Castillos, killed 78 and took 68 prisoners. Only Chief Nana and 17 others escaped. Another 15 Apaches were not in the battle because they were off on a raiding party.

To this day, Apaches believe that Victorio fell on his own knife rather than die at the hands of the Mexicans, who almost certainly would have tortured him to death over many days.

Many Apache women and children died fighting; very typical of encounters with American and Mexican soldiers. The old people were shot; young Apache women captives raped. The surviving Apache women and children were sold into slavery.

Knowing the survivors would need her help, Lozen immediately leaves the Mescalero Reservation to help her people who had sought safety in the high, rugged Sierra Madre that divides Chihuahua and Sonora Mexico. She rode alone south across the desert, somehow making her way undetected through U.S. and Mexican cavalries camped at every known water hole. She rejoins the decimated band, now led by the ancient and crippled, Nana.

1881: Nana's Revenge

Lozen fought along side Nana and his 40 remaining warriors as they engaged in a two-month, thousand-mile-long bloody campaign across southwestern New Mexico to avenge Victorio's death and the slaughter and enslavement of their people. They kill about 50 White-Eyes, steal over 200 horses and mules, all the while being chased by more than a thousand U.S. soldiers and militiamen.

Nana says of Lozen, "Though she is a woman, there is no warrior more worthy than the sister of Victorio."

Many say that the Mexican army never would have achieved their surprise ambush at Tres Castillos if Victorio's younger sister had been there. Her people believed she had the Power to know, not only when the enemy was near, but their strength, and from which direction they would attack.

On September 3, 1886, Chief Naiche and Geronimo surrendered 24 men and 14 women and children to General Miles. Lozen was among the newly minted prisoners-of-war. They had fought until they had no more to fight with. Moreover their families had already been shipped to Florida and this last little group of hostiles missed their families terribly. So they agreed to exile in Florida (a place they could not imagine) for two years, at which time they would all be returned to their ancestral homelands in New Mexico and Arizona.

Dahteste

Dahteste (1860 – 1955)

As extraordinary as Lozen's story is, she was not the lone Chiricahua woman warrior. She had a companion, Dahteste (pronounced Tah-des-te). Unlike Lozen who never married, Dahteste was married and had children. But her people remember Dahteste more as a great hunter and warrior. Moreover, she was fluent in English, a skill often helpful to her people when negotiating with the White-Eyes.

Dahteste spent 3 years on the warpath with Geronimo and she was with Lozen when they surrendered to General Miles. Her people say she was more delicate and feminine than Lozen, but no less deadly.

Nearly all Chiricahua Apaches, more than 400, including Lozen and Dahteste, and the Chiricahua scouts who helped the U.S. Army subdue them, were shipped by railroad from their homeland in Arizona to military prisons in Florida. There Dahteste survived pneumonia and tuberculosis, two virulent diseases that decimated her people while confined in crowded, unsanitary old forts.

A few years later, after they had been transferred to that miserable swamp called Mt. Vernon Barracks in Alabama, her best friend Lozen died from TB while they were still prisoners-of-war. Lozen was buried there in an unmarked grave.

Many years later, all captive Chiricahuas were transferred to Fort Sill Oklahoma, where conditions for the Apaches were far better than at Mount Vernon Barracks.

In 1913, after 27 years of internment, first in Florida, then Alabama, and finally Oklahoma, the Government freed the surviving 300 or so Chiricahuas and gave them the choice to remain at Fort Sill Oklahoma or move to the Mescalero Apache Reservation in New Mexico. Dahteste chose Mescalero.

That is where author Eve Ball interviewed Dahteste at her New Mexico home when this warrior woman was very old. According to Ball, "Dahteste to the end of her life mourned Lozen." Dahteste outlived Lozen by 65 years.

Colorization of the "only" monochrome known photo of Lozen. – By Wakiya

A Most Extraordinary Presidential Inaugural Parade

Theodore Roosevelt, often referred to simply as TR, was a highly successful American politician, statesman, author, explorer, soldier, naturalist, and reformer ... this latter much to the chagrin of the rich and powerful; particularly J.P. Morgan, John D. Rockefeller; and Andrew Carnegie ... not to mention the political bosses of his day.

As President McKinley's Vice President, Theodore Roosevelt became the 26th President of the United States of America in 1901 when McKinley was assassinated. TR was a man of enormous energy and foresight. For instance, we have him to thank for our National Parks. As with all great men, he was also a man of many faults; chief of which was unbounded arrogance and the uncanny ability to hold a grudge over the slightest disagreement, as he did with his (former) best friend, Howard Taft (TR's successor and future Chief Justice of the Supreme Court).

However, among those faults was not a lack of showmanship or stagecraft. President Roosevelt won the presidency on his own merit in the election of November 1904. His inauguration occurred in March, 1905. His presidency lasted until 1909.

It was TR's capacity as showman, the ability to strike a serious point on a grand scale, that resulted in the most extraordinary Presidential Inaugural Parade ever before or since. Participating in the Parade were 35,000 individuals, but the size of the procession was not what made it so unique.

It was this. At the head of his parade down Pennsylvania Avenue, TR placed 6 incredible individuals who represented a conquered people ... the American Indian.

- Quanah Parker, Comanche • Buckskin Charlie, Ute
- Hollow Horn Bear, Brulé Sioux
- American Horse, Oglala Lakota • Little Plume, Blackfeet

And leading them all on his finest war-pony was the 76-year-old Chiricahua Apache medicine man from Arizona; well-known throughout the nation as "the worst Indian who ever lived"... the indomitable Geronimo. Along the Parade route, as the Indians approached, gasps of surprise and awe were heard from the huge crowd, then uproarious applause and cheers.

Of all the North American tribes that fought the White-Eyes to secure their land and their freedom, Geronimo and his band of Chiricahua Apache warriors, women & children, 39 in all, were the last to surrender to the United States.

In the end, September 1886, it took General Miles' army, 5,000 strong, plus hundreds of Army Indian scouts; and thousands of Mexican soldiers and their Tarahumara scouts; not to mention dozens of civilian militias, to run Geronimo to ground.

For their stubborn resistance ... for embarrassing the armies of two nations and militias of four states for a quarter-century ... the Chiricahua Apaches were given the most severe punishment of any American Indian tribe ... exile to hellholes called Fort Marion and Fort Pickens, Florida, and Mount Vernon, Alabama. There the last remnants of the Chiricahua people began dying from diseases, malnutrition, and hopelessness. Prisoners of the United States government for 27 years, the survivors were never allowed to return to Southeastern Arizona, their ancestral homeland.

Geronimo selling his bows & arrows at the 1904 World's Fair in St. Louis.

None of the six Indians at the head of the great procession had any love for the White-Eyes. They were all participating in the Inaugural Parade for their own purposes. Each wanted access to high-government officials to argue for better treatment of their people.

After receiving a roar of applause during the parade, Geronimo later visited the president in his office and pleaded with Roosevelt to let his people go back to their home in Arizona.

"The ropes have been on my hands for many years and we want to go back to our home," he told the president. Roosevelt responded through an interpreter, "When you lived in Arizona, you had a bad heart and killed many of my people. We will have to wait and see how you act."

Geronimo tried to object but he was silenced by the Commissioner of Indian Affairs, Francis Leupp, who led him out of the president's office. "I did not finish what I wished to say," he told Leupp, according to an article in the *New York Tribune*.

Leupp told Geronimo that he and his people were "better off" in Oklahoma. Certainly the people of Arizona did not want the Chiricahuas back. And had the Chiricahuas returned to Arizona, White mobs would have hung Geronimo. Of this TR was well aware.

Though he patronizingly described Geronimo as an example of a "good Indian," Leupp remained unsympathetic to his requests.

When Geronimo died in 1909 he was still a prisoner-of-war at Fort Sill, OK. In his obituary, the *New York Times* wrote:

"Geronimo gained a reputation for cruelty and cunning never surpassed by that of any other American Indian chief."

True, Geronimo and the Chiricahua Apache warriors he led, were responsible for the deaths of thousands of American and Mexican civilians ... men, women and children; not to mention hundreds of American and Mexican soldiers. But it was war-to-the-death and everybody knew it. By today's standards, all sides committed war crimes.

Even today, Americans and Mexicans seldom consider that in Geronimo's time, we were the invaders and aggressors, not the Apaches. Before it was our land, it was their land. Like all American Indian lands, our forefathers of European stock took it by conquest.

In the New York Times obituary, there was no mention of Geronimo's celebrity at various international expositions; or his role in the recent inauguration; or his strenuous efforts as a medicine man to heal his sick and injured people; or the dedication in his 1906 autobiography that reads:

"Because he has given me permission to tell my story; because he has read that story and knows I try to speak the truth; because I believe that he is fair-minded and will cause my people to receive justice in the future; and because he is chief of a great people, I dedicate this story of my life to Theodore Roosevelt, President of the United States."

No Native American warrior worked so tirelessly, or fought so long, for the dignity and freedom of his people in the only way he knew how until the end of his days.

Tucson's Dirty History

Told by Those that Lived It:
Voices From Tucson's Past: 1716 to 1858

Throughout the recorded history of Tucson, people who lived here, and others who were just traveling through, occasionally recorded their impressions. These hardy pioneers left us with a way to peak into our past though a tiny knothole in time.

Many of their comments reveal the attitudes and prejudices they brought with them to the Old Pueblo. Perhaps from their chronicles we can attain a deeper sense of what living here was really like before the railroad (1880), automobile (1899), and air conditioning (1930's).

Early 1700's

In 1716, Fr. Luis Velarde described the native inhabitants living along the perennially flowing Santa Cruz River. He referred to them as the "Papago", a Spanish corruption of a Pima word that means "bean people" or "bean eater". (The Papago have since officially changed their name to Tohono O'odham, meaning Desert People.) "[*They were*] *of good height and well featured.*" "*[They] lived in harmony together*" and were "*valiant and daring*". We can reasonably presume that the descriptions "valiant and daring" relate to the Papagos many battles to drive off raiding Apaches. The Papagos were not pushovers. Sometimes they gave the raiders a good thrashing.

Fr. Velarde then went on to write, with some disgust, that the Papago practiced plural marriage and easy divorce.

He referred to their religious ceremonies as *"magic"*. The Papago had their myths about a great flood and a savior, he wrote, but: *"It is a long history full of a thousand stupidities..."*

He also complained about their occasional ritual drunkenness, but admitted it lasted *"only for two or three days"* when the cactus fruit ripened.

His final contemptuous comment was that the Papago were *"dull".* It may help us to better understand the Spanish attitude toward our Papagos, Pimas (now Akimel O'otham or River People), Yaquis, and other American Aborigines when we understand that the Spanish intent was to convert, civilize, and then exploit them. Should the Spanish be unable to accomplish this transformation of the Indians, as was the case of the Yaquis, their alternative strategy was usually to try to exterminate them. No doubt it helped ease their conscience, such as it was, by rationalizing that the Indians were physically strong, but superstitious, dimwitted, and thus inferior.

1750's

Not surprisingly, the Papago did not take kindly to Spanish attitudes of innate superiority, and utter disrespect for their Native American customs and religion. In 1757, a German Jesuit named Father Gottfried Bernhardt Middendorff served the Church in an Indian settlement a few miles north of San Xavier del Bac near Tucson. His service here lasted only four months.

"I was fond of my catechumans and they reciprocated my affection with gifts of birds' eggs and wild fruit. But our mutual

contentment did not last long because in the following May (1757) we were attacked in the night by about five hundred savage heathens and had to withdraw as best we could. I with my soldiers and various families fled to Mission San Xavier del Bac were we arrived at daybreak."

1760's

Not all of the Catholic missionaries looked down on the Natives. We get a vivid description from Father Pedro Font of one priest who actually liked the Indians. It was written in the late 1760's.

"Father Garces is so well suited to get along with the Indians and among them that he appears to be but an Indian himself. Like the Indians, he is impassive in everything. He sits with them in the circle, or at night around the fire, with his legs crossed. There he will sit musing two or three hours or more, oblivious to all else, talking with much serenity and deliberation. And though the foods of the Indians are as nasty and dirty as those outlandish people themselves, the father eats them with great gusto, and says they are good for the stomach and delicious. In short, God has created him, as I see it, solely for the purpose of seeking out these unhappy, ignorant, and rustic people." (Note: good Father Garces was killed in 1781 in an Indian uprising at Yuma Crossing.)

1770's

Despite almost constant war with the Apaches, by 1777, Tucson was a growing settlement of 77 persons of European descent on the far northwest frontier of New Spain. By 1804, that population had multiplied to 300. By 1819, Tucson had a population of 500 ... counting only Spaniards, of course.

Early 1800's

However, a 1804 report by Tucson Presidio Commandant Zuniga stated that, counting everyone, Spaniards, Indians, and mestizos (those of mixed Spanish and American Indian ancestry of which there were many), Tucson's population was 1,015.

For decades, the Apaches did their best, not merely to make sure that this would be as big as Tucson would ever get, but to actually drive all foreigners from the land they claimed for themselves. They almost succeeded.

In 1873, former governor Safford and merchant pioneer Sam Hughes interviewed long-time Tucson resident Mariana Diaz for the Arizona Citizen. At the time, Señora Diaz was over 100 years old. According to the article, *"She referred to the pleasant times they used to have, when their wants were few and easily supplied, and told how they danced and played and enjoyed themselves."*

In the article, she mentions that crime was almost unknown, but mescal was plentiful. *"But it was only on rare occasion that they drank to excess, and then they acted to each other like brothers."*

According to Señora Diaz, if it had not been for the Apaches, *"they would not have known what trouble was."* She said that her husband and many relatives had died as a result of Indian attacks. (Arizona Citizen: June 21, 1873)

Mid-1800's

By 1843, the presidios at Tubac and Tucson were in deplorable condition. The Tucson convento, a large fortified mission structure on the west bank of the Santa Cruz near present-day Mercado San Agustín at the corner of Congress St. and Avenida del Convento, was abandoned. The orchards and fields were hardly tended any more. Why? In addition to almost continuous pressure from Apaches, European diseases had decimated the local native population. Mestizo was the only growing demographic. The communities of San Xavier and Tucson were barely surviving.

A Time of Change

Life in Tucson began to change in 1848. Gold had been discovered in California that year, and over the next two years, tens of thousands of Anglo-America '49'ers made their way west through this little Mexican village. Some recorded their impressions.

John Durivage was a reporter with the New Orleans Daily Picayunne when he first saw Tucson in 1849. He wrote that he was surprised by the "solemn grandeur" of the church at Bac. He also commented on the *"bright and intelligent Indians" and the "rich and fertile land"* along the Santa Cruz. But, Tucson was *"a miserable place garrisoned by about one hundred men."*

Perhaps we "modern" Tucsonans can best empathize with his assessment of the weather. He said it was HOT! So hot, he wrote, that the pores *"are now reopened and perspiration flows at the slightest exertion."*

Durivage also commented that many Mexican women and Indians came to their camp *"all eager to traffic and anxious to buy needles and thread."* He described the local settled Apaches as *"cowardly and imbecile"* ... *"a degraded and miserable set"* ... *"[exhibiting] that particularly squalid and filthy appearance usual when the wild man leaves his native hills, casts off his old habits and pursuits, and hovers around the haunts of civilization."*

We can reasonably imagine that, had Durivage come across the Apaches led by Cochise and later Geronimo living free in the wilds of the Chiricahua Mountains, he might have employed a somewhat different set of adjectives.

In 1852, John Bartlett arrived in Tucson. He was the American commissioner who, in 1849 along with his Mexican counterpart, had been charged with establishing the new official border between the two countries following the end of the Mexican War.

Upon his arrival, he sketched a picture of Tucson from Sentinel Peak ("A" Mountain). He noted that the town's population could not be more than 300 souls. He blamed the lack of population on the Apaches. Bartlett quickly became aware of what every resident knew and feared. Tucson was surrounded by a hostile desert controlled by even more hostile Apaches.

The Apaches, he wrote, had forced the region's ranchers and farmers to abandon their crops and herds and move to either Tucson or Tubac for protection. If this dusty, dirty little Mexican town was to survive, something had to be done.

However, given his description of Tucson, we can wonder if he thought the effort to solve the Apache problem would be worthwhile.

Gadsden Purchase

With the Gadsden Purchase of 1854, the United States purchased, for $10 million, about 30,000 square miles that is now Southern New Mexico and Southern Arizona from the Rio Grande to the California border.

It would be two years, 1856, before a contingent of U.S. forces could take control of Tucson. As per agreement, about two-dozen Mexican soldiers stayed on to protect the town until an orderly transfer of power could be arranged.

An article in the San Francisco Weekly Chronicle dated November 14, 1856 mentioned that the last departing 26 Mexican soldiers of the Presidio had *"persuaded some of the native families to accompany them [south of the new International Border] to avoid the brutal treatment and other numerous evils ... inflicted on the Spanish race whenever the former [American Anglos] has the upper hand."*

However, many years later in an interview with the Arizona Historical Society, longtime Tucson resident, Carmen Lucero, recalled: *"I have often heard my mother say that the coming of the Americans was a Godsend to Tucson, for the Indians had killed off many of the Mexicans and the poor were being ground down by the rich. The day the [U.S.] troops took posses-*

sion, there was lots of excitement. They raised the [American] flag on the [Presidio] wall and the people welcomed them with a fiesta and they were all on good terms. We felt alive after the Americans took possession and times were more profitable."

Note: In the 19th century, Tucson was the only walled city in America.

1858

Tucson by 1858 was beginning to see Americans elected to public office, although out of a population of about 200, there were only a dozen or so American Anglos. It was the Americans who began building roads sufficient for stagecoaches and wagon trains. Tucson was becoming a transportation hub on the route from San Antonio to San Diego. Times were definitely changing.

Phocion Way from Ohio was an employee of the Santa Rita Mining Company. In June, 1858, he arrived in Tucson via the San Antonio and San Diego Mail Line. Because passengers and mail had to travel by muleback between Yuma and San Diego, this short-lived enterprise was more generally known as the Jackass Mail. Way quickly pronounced Tucson a "miserable place". Of course, those of us living in Tucson today would probably use the same description if we had to travel by mule in June, our hottest, driest month. Perhaps more so if we had to endure summers without air conditioning.

He wrote that he found the few Americans here "pleasant and entertaining". But that was about the only good thing he had to say about the place.

"There is a small creek [that] runs through town. The water is alkaline and warm. The hogs wallow in the creek, the Mexicans water their asses and cattle and wash themselves and their clothes and drink water out of the same creek. The Americans have dug a well and procure tolerably good water ... which they use."

There is no tavern or other accommodation here for travelers, and I was obliged to roll myself in my blanket and sleep either in the street or in the corral, as the station house has no windows or floor and was too close and warm. The corral is where they keep their horses and mules, but I slept very comfortably as the ground was made soft by manure. I would rather have slept in the street as a great many natives do, but it is hardly safe for a stranger. Someone might suppose that he had money about his person and quietly stick a knife into him, and no one would be the wiser – there is no law here, or if there is, it is not enforced. Might makes right."

He wrote about two Anglos, a man named Batch who was shot to death by a man named Fryer. *[The killer] is running at large and no particular notice is taken of it. I guess King Alcohol was at the bottom of the trouble."*

The Native Women of Tucson

Way also found the local women of interest. *"Among the native women here I believe that chastity is a virtue unknown. Some of the young girls are pretty. They are remarkable for the ease and grace of their movements and their brilliant black eyes. Some of them are very bold. They have a great fancy for Americans and a greaser stands no chance with a white man. They are generally tenderhearted and humane and in sickness are noted for being good and faithful nurses.*

Nearly every man in our mail party seems to have a lover here, and when the mail arrives they are always at the station to welcome them. One of our party named Beardsley seems to be a great favorite of the senoritas, and has a fine looking black-eyed girl for his special favorite. He is laying on the ground within six feet of me at this moment fast asleep, while she is sitting by his side keeping the flies from disturbing him."

Primary source: *Tucson: The Life and Times of an American City*; by C. L. Sonnichsen. University of Oklahoma Press; 1982, 1987. An extensively annotated history, very well-written, with many historical illustrations. If you would like

The Camp Grant Massacre: Prologue To A Tragedy

Camp Grant 1870's

How Tucson's Wealthiest & Most Prominent Leaders Committed Mass Murder & Got Away With It.

Today, there's nothing there. Nothing to suggest what happened in the early morning of April 30, 1871. Nothing to commemorate this blood-soaked ground where between 118 and 144 people, almost all women and children, lay murdered and mutilated. The actual number will never be known with certainty.

Camp Grant, named for the famous Civil War general, was an Army post built at the confluence of the San Pedro River and Aravaipa Creek about 70 miles northeast of Tucson. It was located here in the late 1860's so that U.S. soldiers could better protect local settlers and miners who had begun to flood into this area near present-day Winkelman. This had been the home to Aravaipa & Pinal Apaches (aka Western Apaches) for centuries.

The post was first constructed in 1860 to deal with the "Apache Problem". Between 1860 and 1873, the post was abandoned or destroyed and then rebuilt multiple times, and it was known by a variety of names, starting with Fort Breckinridge in 1860 before becoming Camp Grant in 1866.

From this vantage point, the Army hoped it would also be in good position to protect the San Pedro River overland freight route that ran from New Mexico to California from bands of Western Apaches.

Apaches: Hated and Feared

These Aravaipa & Pinal Apaches had few friends among other nearby tribes. Long before the coming of the Spanish, Mexicans, and then the Anglo-Americans, these Western Apaches had raided other Indian groups and were hated by their neighbors, including the Papago Indians we now call Tohono O'odham or Desert People.

When the Spanish, and later the Mexicans and Americans, began to settle in Southern Arizona, the Western Apaches were happy to raid their ranches, mining camps, settlements, stagecoaches, and wagon trains. Raiding was how they supplemented their seasonal subsistence practices that included hunting, gathering and some farming, particularly in Aravaipa Canyon.

To be a respected Apache male, you had to be a successful raider, which meant you had to be a skilled thief and murderer. To the Apache mind, however, raiding was always morally justified. First, it was often the only logical way to keep their families from starving. And second, they could always justify their raids because the people they stole from were classified as enemies. They didn't consider it murder to kill enemies. Of course, today, neither do we.

It's important for us to understand that the onslaught of American and Mexican farmers, ranchers, merchants, and miners steadily displaced these Aravaipa & Pinal Apaches so that they lost their best seasonal hunting, gathering, and farming lands. The more the settlers' very presence displaced these Apaches, the more the Apaches had to rely on raiding for survival. The invaders were not interested in understanding how they were contributing to the "Apache Problem". They were here in Southern Arizona to make their fortunes in this "new" land. And they were not about to allow "savages" to spoil their opportunities if they could help it.

President Grant

Generally, the raiding Apaches were after anything they believed would benefit themselves, particularly horses, mules, and ammunition, but also items they could trade, such as slaves, for whiskey and better weapons. They were utterly unconcerned about "The Others". The Apaches excelled at lightening fast ambushes and seldom left their victims alive.

It took the Army a quarter of a century (1861-1886) to solve the "Apache Problem", which they accomplished by both military force and treachery (aka lies and broken treaties). The Apache Wars, not the U.S. armed conflict in Afghanistan, was America's longest war.

Anyone living in Southern Arizona and Southern New Mexico or Northern Sonora and Chihuahua Mexico who wasn't Apache was rightly terrified of them. When confronted with a superior force, such as the U.S. Cavalry, the Apaches were adept at guerrilla warfare. From the time of the Camp Grant Massacre in 1871, it would be another 15 years before the legendary Chiricahua Apache shaman and war leader, Geronimo, would surrender for the 4th and final time.

Very few Anglos or Mexicans at the time saw themselves as invaders and the root cause of ever-escalating raiding and reprisals. John Clum, Indian Agent and later publisher/editor of the Tombstone Epitaph, was one of the few. President Ulysses S. Grant was another.

President Grant's Peace Policy

Prior to and immediately after the Civil War (1861-65), the Americans had adopted the "Mexican Policy" toward the Apaches: assimilation through marriage or extermination. To increase civilian motivation to achieve extermination, bounties were offered on Apache scalps. If you had the scalp of an Apache baby, the government would pay you $25, serious money in those days. Souvenir trophies, such as teeth beaten out of living Apache women, were popular. And worse.

However, this utterly brutal, wantonly barbaric approach to "The Apache Problem" wasn't working out as planned. The enormous size and ruggedness of the terrain and the cunning and resilience of the Apaches were more than a match for the limited resources of the U.S. Army.

When U.S. Grant became President of the United States in 1869, he considered a better, more affordable and effective policy. For starters, he listened to many influential voices of the Eastern Establishment, including Vincent Colyer who served on the Board of Indian Commissioners.

"The peaceable relations of the Apaches with the Americans continued until the latter adopted the Mexican theory of "extermination" and by acts of inhuman treachery and cruelty made them our implacable foes: that this policy has resulted in a war which, in the last ten years, has cost us a thousand lives and over forty millions of dollars, and the country is no quieter nor the Indians any nearer extermination than they were at the time of the Gadsden Purchase [1854] ... these Indians still beg for peace, and all of them can be placed on reservations and fed at an expense of less than half a million of dollars a year, without loss of life."

Soon the President decreed what became known as the "Grant Peace Policy". It included several key provisions, among them:

Camp Grant Massacre - Prologue

• **Reservations.** If Apaches surrendered and agreed never again to raid, they would be given reservation lands upon which they could provide for themselves, initially with the help of the Government.

• **Rations.** The peaceful Apaches would be given sufficient rations to sustain themselves until they could become self-sufficient; a year or so of adequate food & clothing, planting seed, farm implements, livestock, etc.

• **Protection.** As essentially prisoners-of-war, the U.S. Army would protect the Apaches from civilian violence; a particularly ugly fact of life at the time. American & Mexican settlers generally considered any Apache, man, woman, or child, vermin to be killed on sight. It mattered not at all if the Apaches had surrendered and were at peace.

• **Conversion.** If the Apaches would convert to Christianity, all the better for friendly relations.

The Economics of the Apache Wars

The "Grant Peace Policy" was not born of solely humanitarian considerations. It also intended to reduce the incredibly high cost of maintaining an Army in the field so far from civilization. If the Apaches were pacified and became self-sufficient, the many forts scattered about Southern Arizona would no longer be necessary. Nor would the services of those Tucson merchants and ranchers who sold food & supplies to the Army at exorbitant prices.

Also, with the Apaches pacified and self-sufficient and the forts abandoned, the opportunities for rampant graft and corruption would dry up. Just as bad, if the Apaches were successful at raising crops and livestock, they could become formidable competitors to the Anglo and Mexican farmers and ranchers.

Rampant Corruption

By the time U.S. Grant became President, top military and

civilian officials understood that the Army and the Bureau of Indian Affairs in Southern Arizona were notoriously corrupt.

According to University of Arizona professor, Ian Record:

"Rampant graft and corruption further hampered the limited military might that the army wielded against Apaches. Calculating politicians, scheming contractors, and underhanded Indian agents in Arizona routinely fleeced the government, depriving Apaches on peaceful terms of truce-guaranteed supplies. Often, desperately needed provisions never reached posts and feeding stations because of bureaucratic incompetence, or outright theft. Frequently, Indian agents simply sold the rations and equipment designated for Apaches and kept the proceeds. In addition, some army officers "diverted supplies to civilian merchants and pocketed the money. The same equipment and supplies sometimes were resold to the Indian Service or army quartermasters. Civilian contractors took advantage of the opportunity to reap excessive profits." (from Big Sycamore Stands Alone)

Apache "Feeding Stations"

During this time, one small Apache band after another surrendered as pressure from settlers and the Army increased and the number of warriors declined from old age, but more often death in battle. The Apache Wars were, after all, wars of attrition. Following surrender, most were sent to reservations where sickness (particularly malaria, but also smallpox), malnutrition, exposure, and hopelessness further reduced their numbers.

The Army's Apache Policy: 1870

In 1870, in accordance with the Grant Peace Policy, General George Stoneman, the commander of the Army in Arizona Territory, established "feeding stations" to provide rations for those Apaches who surrendered. By doing so, the Army hoped to convince all "renegade" Apaches to cease raiding and accept reservation life. Stoneman's Apache policy, the practical application of the Grant Peace Policy, intended to give the Apaches sufficient food, farm implements, seed, agricultural training, livestock, and adequate fertile land so that in a year or two the peaceful Apaches would be self-sufficient and therefore have no reason to raid upon what was quickly becoming an onslaught of Anglo and Mexican settlers into Apacheria, including all of Southwestern New Mexico and Southeastern Arizona.

Soon, many Apache bands indicated a willingness to give up raiding and adopt a sedentary lifestyle in return for adequate rations, the means to become self-sufficient, and protection for civilian violence.

Lt. Royal Whitman and Chief Eskiminzin

In February 1871, five old, hungry Pinal Apache women in ragged clothes came to Camp Grant looking for a son of one of the women who had been taken prisoner. The senior commander, Lt. Royal Whitman, had just arrived from the east and had not yet learned to hate all Apaches.

He fed these women, treated them kindly, and sent them off with a promise of similar treatment for others of their band if they would come to

Chief Eskiminzin

Camp Grant in peace. Word spread and other Apaches from Aravaipa and Pinal bands soon came to the post seeking rations of beef and flour. Among them was a young Apache war chief named Eskiminzin (aka Hashke' Bahnzin) who told Lt. Whitman that he and his small band were tired of war and wanted to settle on nearby Aravaipa Creek where the ground was fertile and there was plenty of water for successful farming.

In return for rations, Chief Eskiminzin and his Apaches

Aravaipa Creek Today

turned over most of their weapons to Lt. Whitman and promised to stop raiding. Whitman accepted their promise and, in addition to rations, offered them pay for field work.

As more Apaches arrived, Whitman created a refuge or "rancheria" along Aravaipa Creek about a half mile east of Camp Grant, and wrote to his superior for instructions. Due to pompous bureaucratic officiousness, no reply was forthcoming.

By early March there were 300 Aravaipa and Pinal Apaches camped near Camp Grant. By March's end there were 500.

During March, however, the flow of Aravaipa Creek declined and Lt. Whitman authorized the Arivaipa and Pinal Apaches to move five miles upstream from Camp Grant, to the mouth of Aravaipa Canyon, portions of which today are jointly owned and managed by the BLM and Nature Conservancy.

(Note: You can hike through Aravaipa Canyon today if you have a permit. Watch out for bears, lions, and monsoon floods. SouthernArizonaGuide.com has more information and many photographs about Aravaipa Canyon.)

Camp Grant Massacre: The Killers

Fear, Anger, and Greed In Tucson

Some seventy miles south of Aravaipa Canyon in the small, dusty, predominantly Mexican town of Tucson, the residents had conflicted feelings toward the soldiers stationed at Camp Grant, and the military commander of the Territory, General Stoneman.

On the one hand, the citizens of Tucson felt surrounded by a vast desert controlled by Apaches who continued to raid and murder despite the growing presence of the Army. They blamed the Army for not keeping American citizens safe. Truth-be-told, most Anglo and Mexican residents of Southern Arizona, and their influential newspapers, were at this time demanding that the Army simply exterminate all Apaches, rather than feed and clothe them. Almost every Tucsonan believed that feeding the Apaches actually enabled, even encouraged more raiding.

Moreover, the San Pedro River overland freight route guarded by the Camp Grant soldiers was taking business from the valuable overland route that went through Tucson.

On the other hand, many Tucson businessmen were profiting handsomely from the experimental Apache "feeding stations" operated by the soldiers. They were also profiting by providing substantial supplies, including a lot of beef, for the maintenance of the soldiers at Camp Grant and other forts around Southern Arizona. Then, as now, Tucson's biggest source of wealth by far was the Government of the United States.

Yet, if the Army was successful in teaching the Apaches to be self-sufficient farmers, as was their goal, the military posts all around Arizona would be disbanded and this lucrative trade would dry up. The most prominent and prosperous Tucson merchants & ranchers were making fortunes selling to the Government. These locals included: Samuel

Hughes, Hiram Stevens, Edward Nye Fish, Sidney DeLong, Jesus Maria Elias, William Oury. A.P.K. Safford, William Zuckendorf, and John Wasson.

Thus, many Tucsonans were motivated by their personal economic interests to foment trouble between the Army and the Apaches. War was good for business. Peace, not so much. In this regard, not much has changed in the past 140-some years.

In early 1871, as the population of peaceful Pinal and Araviapa Apaches continued to grow near Camp Grant, other Apaches, most notably the Chiricahuas led by Cochise and Geronimo, continued to raid and slaughter Anglo and Mexican settlers throughout Southern Arizona.

The good citizens of Tucson considered these raids and atrocities related to the Camp Grant experiment, even though there was ample evidence at the time that the Aravaipa and Pinal Apaches at Camp Grant were not involved.

At the time, John Wasson, editor of the *Tucson Citizen*, claimed in repeated editorials that the government uses the Apache reservations and feeding stations to: *"... fatten up the savages so they would be in better shape to murder American citizens."*

Motivated by fear, anger, and greed, bellicose meetings were held to determine a course of action. Later, no one would accuse the Tucson civic leaders of being indecisive.

Tucson's Public Safety Committee

First, they formed the Public Safety Committee and sent Territorial Governor Safford to Washington to lobby President Grant and General Sherman for more troops and General Stoneman's removal. Then they meticulously planned the annihilation of the Camp Grant Apaches to ensure that the reservation policy would fail and the Apache Wars would continue to enrich the good citizens of Tucson.

Wasson

However, before they could act, they had to incite unfettered hatred of all Apaches to recruit the necessary manpower and raise sufficient funds for the planned campaign. That duty fell to John Wasson, editor of the *Tucson Citizen,* at the time the most read newspaper in the Territory, primarily because of Wasson's anti-Apache - anti-Army rants. Wasson was to the Tucson Public Safety Committee what Joseph Goebbles was to Adolph Hitler; Minister of Propaganda.

In editorials and supposedly objective news reports, Wasson repeatedly aroused public passions against all Apaches, exaggerating, sensationalizing, and inventing accounts of their thievery and atrocities.

Moreover, Wasson vilified 37-year-old First Lieutenant Royal Emerson Whitman who had taken command of Camp Grant earlier in the year. In part, the antipathy between the newspaper editor and the ranking officer was because Whitman was new to the Territory and did not harbor sufficient bigotry and hatred of all Apaches. In fact, Whitman, a competent officer, exhibited kindness toward those Apaches who surrendered and took up farming.

Lt. Whitman

Wasson invariably pointed to the Aravaipa and Pinal Apaches under the protection of the Army at Camp Grant as the culprits, even though Lt. Whitman, counting the Apache males every second or third day, made it impossible for them to have conducted the distant raids south of Mission San Xavier that Wasson and others accused them of committing without Whitman knowing of their extended absence.

Wasson and the other ringleaders knew this ... and ignored the evidence for their own purposes. In late April 1871, the Public Safety Committee became an avenging mob.

Note: In 1870, John Wasson was appointed Surveyor General at a time when most of Southern Arizona, including Tucson, had not yet been officially surveyed. Which means, real estate property boundaries had not been officially established. If you thought you owned real estate in Tucson or anywhere else in Southern Arizona, it would have been a smart business decision to make John Wasson your dearest friend.

The Mob

In the afternoon of April 28, 1871, an excited mob of 6 Anglos and 48 Mexicans left Tucson for Camp Grant, along with 94 Papago warriors. The Papago had easily been recruited from their reservation just south of Tucson at San Xavier Mission. They were traditional enemies of the Pinal and Aravaipa Apache with whom they had a long history of war. Like all the settled residents of Southern Arizona, the Papago hated and feared the Apaches.

Note: the Papago Indians are now called what they had always called themselves, Tohono O'odham, meaning Desert People. ". "Papago" is a Spanish corruption of a Pima word that means "bean people" or "bean eater".

The Ring Leaders

Gov. Safford

Safford

In the months that proceeded the Massacre, Territorial Governor Safford secured the best repeating rifles and ammunition from the U.S. Government and had them delivered to prominent Tucson merchant, Sam Hughes. Although he did not participate in the actual murders, Safford's involvement encouraged the mob because they knew there would be no legal ramifications from the Territorial government.

Hughes

By 1871, Sam Hughes was a successful Tucson businessman with primary interests in livestock & mining. His biggest customer by far? The U.S. Army. He had already been appointed to the post of Adjutant General of Arizona Territory by Governor Safford.

On the morning of April 28, Hughes provided the modern weapons only to the Americans and Mexicans. It was, after all, illegal for a white man to give or sell a gun to an Indian. The Papagos would have to use their traditional weapons; bows and arrows, knives, and war clubs for bashing heads ... a practice at which they were very proficient.

Mr. Hughes, along with merchants Hiram Stevens and William Zuckendorf, also provided wagons supplied with sufficient water and food for the two and a half days it was going to take to get his mob to Aravaipa, kill all the Apaches there, then return to Tucson. Like Safford, Hughes did not participate in the actual murders. He just provided the means.

DeLong

As partner & general manager of Tully & Ochoa, the largest mercantile firm and biggest taxpayer in Southern Arizona, by 1971 Sidney DeLong has amassed a personal fortune supplying Army forts throughout Southern Arizona and then taking his earnings and making even more money speculating in mining and real estate. Tully & Ochoa's most lucrative clients by far? The U.S. Army and the Bureau of Indian Affairs.

Sidney DeLong

Stevens

In 1871, Hiram Stevens was a partner of Sam Hughes in the richly rewarding enterprise of government contracts for grain, beef, and hay. Early on, he did exceptionally well investing in mining. Stevens also owned Tucson's largest butcher shop, an exceedingly profitable business given the Army's insatiable demand for beef. He was wealthy enough to lend money and greedy enough to charge 2% per month. Stevens chaired the Public Safety Committee.

On April 29th, the day before the Massacre, a group of heavily armed members of the Public Safety Committee led by Hiram Stevens blocked all traffic on the road from Tucson to Camp Grant until 7AM on the 30th. Should the mobs movements and plan be discovered, Stevens made certain that no one could get word of their intentions to the 50 or so soldiers at Camp Grant. Surprise was critical to the success of their mission.

Note: That road leading north out of Tucson was called Camp Grant Road and later Old Camp Grant Road. Today we know it as Oracle Road, Tucson's main North-South artery.

On the afternoon of April 29th, the commander at Fort Lowell learned about the planned attack and ordered two soldiers to ride as fast as possible to Camp Grant and warn Lt. Whitman. Stevens and his men "detained" the riders. Had it not been for Hiram Stevens, the Camp Grant soldiers would have been warned about the plot in plenty of time to protect those Apaches farming in Aravaipa Canyon.

Oury
In 1871, William Oury, a former Texas Ranger, owned substantial farming and cattle-grazing land along the Santa Cruz River south of Tucson. Apaches often raided his crop storehouses and stole his cattle. According to Sam Hughes' wife, Atanacia, *"Bill Oury was the leader of them all; he had just lost a fine lot of cattle and was anxious to do something."*

Note: at Adobe Rose Inn B&B (which we highly recommend) innkeepers Marion & Jim Hook have a bedroom dedicated to Atanacia. Interestingly, their inn is located in the Sam Hughes neighborhood of mid-town Tucson.

Elias

By 1871, Jesus Elias was a Tucson councilman (prior to incorporation) who had lost two brothers and a lot of cattle to Apaches raids. His surviving brother, Juan, had been wounded by Apaches several years earlier. With more than 200,000 acres of prime ranch land around Tubac, the brothers were reaping enormous profits from the sale of crops and beef to the Army and Bureau of Indian Affairs. These Mexican brothers were hot to kill Apaches and didn't much care which ones.

Zuckendorf

By 1871, William Zuckendorf, along with his brother Louis and nephew Albert Steinfeld, had established what became the most successful and long-lasting retail business in Arizona. Apache raiding made it difficult for the brothers to get wholesale goods from back east across the desert and into their Tucson retail store. Like the others, the Zuckendorfs, made a fortune from government contracts and, later, investments in mines, including the Copper Queen in Bisbee.

Surprise Attack At Dawn

Just before dawn on April 30, 1871, the Tucson mob mounted a surprise attack on the Pinal and Aravaipa camp. The day before, most of the Apache men had left their women, children, and old men in camp and were up in the mountains hunting or collecting mescal. The mob knew that the Aravaipa & Pinal warriors had surrendered their rifles to Lt. Whitman as a part of the peace agreement. The mob was well aware, with the advantage of surprise at first light, the Apaches would be asleep and defenseless.

The Papago were in the forefront of the attack, clubbing, stabbing, and slashing their nearly helpless victims to death. They also raped and mutilated the young Apache girls. Most of the Anglos and Mexicans positioned themselves on a bluff above the rancheria and shot any Apaches trying to escape the slaughter. Of those who managed to escape, most were men. According to Lt. Whitman's official report:

"Their (Aravaipa & Pinal) camp was surrounded and attacked at daybreak. So sudden and unexpected was it, that no one was awake to give the alarm, and I found quite a number of women shot while asleep beside their bundles of hay which they had collected to bring in that morning.

The wounded who were unable to get away had their brains beaten out with clubs or stones, while some were shot full of arrows after being mortally wounded by gunshot. The bodies were all stripped. Of the whole number buried, one was an old man and one was a well-grown boy - all the rest were women and children. Of the whole number killed or missing, about one hundred and twenty-five, eight only were men.

It has been said (the perpetrators claimed that the men had left camp to raid) that the men were not there - they were all there. On the 28th we counted one hundred and twenty-eight men, a small number being absent of mescal, all of whom have since been in."

Chief Eskiminzin was asleep when the attack began. He and most of his able-bodied, but unarmed men were able to escape by running through thick brush to the surrounding hills. The Chief took his young daughter in his arms and ran. Two of his wives and five of his other children were killed by the O'odham warriors.

The Papago captured about 26 young Apache children. Once the fighting was over, the Papago scalped and mutilated their victims. Most of their young captives were eventually sold into slavery in Sonora, Mexico for $100 a piece.

Six or eight were sold as slaves to prominent families in Tucson. According to Atanacia Santa Cruz Hughes, *"... they brought a lot of little ones into Tucson ... These (Apache) children were divided up among a number of us."*

As soon as Lt. Whitman heard about the Massacre, he sent

a medical team to render assistance, but they found no survivors. He had his soldiers bury the dead Apaches.

The Trial

From the Camp Grant Massacre, the Apaches learned once again that the Americans could not be trusted.

In the East, where American citizens were no longer threatened by Indians, the reaction was outrage. Eastern newspapers demanded justice. President Grant condemned the event as *"purely murder"* and threatened to place Arizona Territory under martial law if the participants were not brought to trail.

The defendents at the trial.

In October, 1871, a grand jury indicted 100 individuals thought to have participated in the massacre. In December, the very public trial lasted 5 days. The attorneys for the defense focused their arguments exclusively on the history of Apache raids, murders, and depredations. No Apaches were invited to testify. The jury deliberated for 19 minutes and declared all defendants not guilty. What was a massacre in the East was justifiable homicide in Tucson.

That year, the new commanding officer in the Arizona Territory, Lt. Col. George Crook, undertook a survey of military posts and potential reservations sites. Crook had Camp Grant closed and ordered a new Fort Grant to be built at the western base of Mount Graham.

In the aftermath of the Massacre, Governor Safford convinced Crook that Lt. Whitman was the problem. Crook had Whitman court-martialed three times based on trumped up charges of drunkenness, philandering, and behavior unbecoming an officer. Whitman beat all charges, and retired from the Army in 1879. Crook, for all of his tenacity and brilliance in defeating the Apaches, continued to believe, despite overwhelming evidence to the contrary, that Whitman was an unfit officer. Lt. Whitman, who had served gallantly in the Civil War, died at age 79 and was buried at Arlington National Cemetery.

Note: The new location in present-day Graham County was better located to subdue the remaining hostiles. In March 1873, Camp Grant at the junction of the San Pedro and Aravaipa Rivers was abandoned. Today, it's the site of Central Arizona College. The new Fort Grant is no longer a military fort, but a location for a state prison.

Immediately following the massacre, a reservation was set aside for the Apaches at Camp Grant. But the following year all Apache reservations were consolidated and moved north to the intersection of the San Carlos and the Gila Rivers ... what became known to the Apaches as the dreaded San Carlos Apache Reservation.

In the years following the massacre, relatives of the enslaved Apache children repeatedly petitioned the U.S. government to help repatriate their kidnapped children. Only 7 or 8 ever returned to their people. Chief Eskiminzin later wrote,

"When I made peace with Lt. Whitman, my heart was very big and happy. The people of Tucson and San Xavier must be crazy. They acted as though they had neither heads nor hearts ... they must have a thirst for our blood. These Tucson people write for the papers and tell their own story. The Apache have no one to tell their story."

Today, the massacre site, about five miles upstream from the abandoned site of Camp Grant on Aravaipa Creek, is unmarked. Some of the descendants of those massacred want a monument placed at the site to commemorate what happened there. Others do not want the exact place marked for fear "pot-hunters" will loot what is now a sacred burial ground to the Aravaipa & Pinal Apaches.

The Rewards Of Mass Murder

The leaders of the Public Safety Committee who participated in or otherwise enabled the Massacre were treated as heroes by everyone in and near Tucson. They all continued to contribute to the good of their community and the City rewarded them by naming streets and places in their honor.

In the years following the Massacre, Bill Oury served as Sheriff of Pima County from 1873 to 1877. The City named a street and a park after him. Hiram Stevens served two terms as Territorial Delegate to the U.S. House of Representatives and then 3 terms in the Arizona Territorial Legislature. In Tucson, Stevens Avenue is named in his honor.

Sam Hughes not only had a street named after him, but an entire Tucson neighborhood. In fact, today the Sam Hughes neighborhood is a National Historic District.

Territorial Governor Safford has a street in Tucson named in his honor, plus an entire city in Southeastern Arizona. The Elias brothers have a Tucson street named for their family. And the tallest peak in the Tucson Mountains is named for John Wasson.

Sidney DeLong was soon elected Mayor of Tucson and later served in the Arizona Territorial Legislature. He has a peak in the Santa Catalina Mountains named in his honor. Interestingly, DeLong was the only leader who, in old age, admitted publicly that he regretted his involvement in the massacre. All the others were defiant and proud to the end.

Note: On Southern Arizona Guide's Tucson History & Libation Walking Tour, we take our tour participants to the homes of some of these "heroes" and share related stories that are just as amazing. For more tour information, go to: SouthernArizonaGuide.com > Guided Tours

Preacher In Helldorado

In the cold Boston winter of 1944-45, Reverend Endicott Peabody was in the final season of his life. At 87 years of age, he had lived perhaps the most productive and influential life of any American clergy. He had much to reflect upon, including 6 months as a young pastor of a little church in a dusty Western mining town that lawman Billy Breakenridge famously referred to as "Helldorado".

Rev. Endicott Peabody

Born into a prominent Massachusetts family, Endicott was primarily educated in England where, in 1880, he graduated from Trinity College, Cambridge with a degree in law. However, he felt a strong and sincere call to the ministry, and in February 1881, became a student at Episcopal Theological School in Cambridge, MA.

Following his first semester, Peabody (pronounced Peabiddie in MA) was asked to take charge of a very small Episcopal congregation in an isolated pocket of Southern Arizona. Six months earlier, the church building had burned to the ground and its priest had moved on. Endicott, known as "Cotty" to friends & family, arrived in Benson, AZ dressed in his finely tailored, but rumpled eastern suit after a 7-day train ride from Boston. There he boarded Sandy Bob's stagecoach for the $2 night ride south, and arrived in Tombstone early on Sunday, January 29, 1882.

If Ever a Town Needed a Preacher

At this time, Tombstone, population about 5,000, was the second largest town in Arizona after Tucson, the former

Allen Street in Tombstone Territory Circa. 1881-1882

capitol of the Territory with a population of about 7,000 (counting only white males registered to vote over the age of 21). Like most mining boomtowns, Tombstone was rough. Along with general stores, butcher shops, a Wells Fargo and telegraph office; restaurants and hotels, an ice cream parlor and a school, Tombstone easily supported over 100 saloons and brothels, including the Bird Cage Theater that the New York Times described as "the wildest, wickedest night spot between Basin Street and the Barbary Coast". Only 4 months earlier, Sandy Bob's stage had been held up and the passengers robbed. Three months earlier, U.S. Deputy Marshal Virgil Earp and his deputies, (Wyatt and Morgan Earp and Dr. John Holliday) had killed Billy Clanton, Frank and Tom McLaury on Fremont Street near the OK Corral. A month earlier, Virgil Earp had survived an assassination attempt, but had lost the use of his left arm.

During Cotty's brief Tombstone tenure, he would find himself, like all Tombstone pioneers, caught up in the feud between the Earps and "The Cowboys". He was there when Morgan Earp was assassinated in March 1882. And he followed the local newspaper accounts and rumors when U.S. Deputy Marshal Wyatt Earp and his posse, including the notorious John (Doc) Holliday, went on a killing spree that became known as the "Earp Vendetta Ride".

Of Morgan Earp's murder, Peabody remarked, *"Murder and revenge have taken place in quick succession and the town is unrestful – feeling that the end will not come until one of the factions is entirely annihilated or leaves the country. Until that occurs we cannot have a town which will attract capitalist or families."*

Building A Church

Cotty was in Tombstone to build a church and expand the Episcopal congregation. This he did by quickly making a lot of friends. He was willing to engage people at every level of Tombstone society wherever they gathered.

The group he most wanted to bring into his congregation

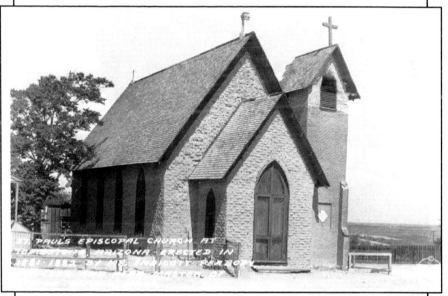

St. Paul's Episcopal Church, Tombstone, AZ circa 1934

was the miners; a rough, mostly illiterate lot to be sure. Once, to get them on his side, Cotty accepted a challenge from a group of miners to take on their champion boxer. The match took place in a smoky saloon that reeked of stale beer, cheap whiskey, and dripping spittoons.

Cotty had been an extraordinary college athlete and was in superb shape. The diarist, George Parsons, described him as *"...quite an athlete and of magnificent build, weighing two hundred pounds, muscles hard as iron."*

But the miners' champion was a huge, powerful man and many in the crowd feared the preacher would be killed. After Cotty knocked the big man to the floor, his swollen face black and blue and bloody, Cotty helped him up and became the miners' hero, bringing many into his growing congregation.

Cotty loved baseball and would happily play catch with anyone. He organized the Tombstone baseball team that would eagerly challenge Bisbee and Tucson teams. Soon after his arrival in Tombstone, the Epitaph, a Tombstone newspaper, wrote: *"Well, we've got a parson who doesn't flirt with the girls, who doesn't drink behind the door, and when it comes to baseball, he's a daisy."*

Churches are always short of funds and fundraising is a principle occupation of any preacher. Cotty was no exception. The completion of the church and a parsonage was going to cost an estimated $5,000 (about $125,000 in 2014 dollars). So Cotty was always fundraising. In the meantime, services were held in the courtroom of the Miners' Exchange, and other venues around town.

Part of Cotty's success at church services was his sincere enthusiasm, the relevance of his message, and the informality of his presentation, as well as his attention to certain accoutrements, including beautiful flowers and a rousing choir. The Tombstone Nugget, rival to the Tombstone Epitaph, wrote on February 18, 1882, *"Talk about muscular*

Christianity. We overheard a miner yesterday say, upon hav-ing the Episcopal minister pointed out to him, "Well, if that lad's argument was a hammer, and religion a drill, he'd knock a hole in the hanging wall of skepticism..." His choir, an all-male quartet including George Parsons, was reportedly the finest in the Territory. On Sunday, February 12th, there were 110 people in the congregation and the collection totaled $25, more than had ever been collected at one service.

Writing in the same month, the Epitaph noted the high atten-dance at both the morning and evening services and that the preacher had delivered *"two very instructive discourses ... in a manner clear and earnest, while the manly bearing of the gentleman lends a decisive force to all his remarks."*

With his easy, friendly manner, Cotty continued his work building up his congregation and raising money for the building fund. On some days, he visited as many as 15 homes to check on the residents well-being, invite them to church and Bible study, or minister to the sick and dying. In Tomb-stone in the early 1880's, *"Death"* visited frequently. For the town's 4 preachers, including Cotty, conducting funeral ser-vices was a routine responsibility.

Sometimes in the evenings he and friends would ride up into the hills west of town just to enjoy the magnificent sun-sets. Nor was it unusual for friends to drop in at the rectory to chat and smoke. George Parsons noted in his diary on March 5, 1882, *"P. likes his claret and a good cigar and I don't see why he shouldn't enjoy them, [even] if he is a minister."*

Once he and friends rode over to Empire Ranch 45 miles northwest just to visit with the Vail family and their ranch hands. On more than one occasion, Cotty rode over to Fort Huachuca to conduct services.

Cotty was not shy about doing the Lord's work. One after-noon he heard that there was a rich poker game going on in one of the saloons among the town's most prominent mining men. At any given moment there was as much as $1,000 in the pot (about $25,000 in 2014 dollars). Cotty walked in, introduced himself, and asked for a donation to help build the church. Eliphalet Gage, general manager of two large mines, counted out $150 from his pile of chips (about $3,750 today) and handed it to the preacher. The others did likewise. Cotty told them he had not expected so much, but assured them that they would not regret their generosity.

In addition to such large individual donations, the Ladies Aid Society put on various fundraising benefits, such as operas and bazaars. The minutes of their meetings show clearly that the biggest block of tickets to raise money for the church building was sold by the saloons.

After two and a half months, the community had raised $4,000 to build the church and another $300 for a parsonage. Construction began in April 1882. According to the Epitaph, the building would *"measure fifty-four by twenty-seven feet".*

On a sweltering July day 1882, his mission accomplished, Endicott Peabody left Tombstone and returned to Massachusetts to complete his seminary studies. George Parsons noted in his diary that day, *"We will not easily fill Peabody's place."*

Miss Francis Peabody

Back in Cambridge, MA, Cotty graduated from the Episcopal Theological School in the spring of 1884. The next year he was ordained an Episcopal priest and, in June 1885, married his childhood sweetheart and cousin, Francis (Fanny) Peabody.

Most famously, in the same year in which he was ordained, Cotty and two colleagues established the Groton School for Boys, a boarding school in Groton, MA near Boston. The Reverend Endicott Peabody served as headmaster for the next 56 years.

In 1889, he founded St. Andrew's Episcopal Church in Ayer, Massachusetts; and also served as a trustee of Lawrence Academy. In 1926, Peabody founded Brooks School. More than a priest, Endicott Peabody was an educator par excellence.

Groton School for Boys

Groton's mission was simple: provide *"intellectual, moral, and physical development" for the sons of America's most elite families."* Under Cotty's leadership, Groton challenged its students to embrace their civil and religious responsibilities. Rev. Peabody declared, in 1884, that *"if some Groton boys do not enter political life and do something for our land it won't be because they have not been urged."*

Each grade consisted of only twenty boys. The annual tuition was $500, twice the annual income of the average American family. Groton accommodations were Spartan; the curriculum demanding. And Peabody was a strict master. Even though his students were from wealthy families (among his students were Theodore Roosevelt's four sons) he refused to allow any them to receive an allowance of more than 25 cents per week.

FDR

In 1896, a fourteen year-old boy from the Hyde Park branch of the elite Roosevelt family of New York became a Groton student. His name was Franklin. He was too small to succeed at Groton's rough & tumble sports. Moreover, Rev. Peabody thought he wasn't particularly bright.

FDR: 18 years of age

St. Paul's - 2015

Nevertheless, Franklin graduated from Groton in 1900 and went on to Harvard, where he graduated with a degree in history in only 3 years. Following Harvard, he studied law at Columbia University, passed the bar in 1907, then practiced law until he went into politics in 1910 when he was elected to the New York State Senate.

In 1905, as he was studying law, Franklin married his cousin, Anna Eleanor Roosevelt, niece of President Theodore Roosevelt. Rev. Peabody officiated at their wedding. When Franklin became President of the United States in 1933, Rev. Peabody led the official prayer service; as he did for three of Franklin's four inaugurations. When they had grown to adulthood, Rev. Peabody officiated at all of Franklin & Eleanor's children's weddings too.

Years later, Franklin said of the good Reverend, *"As long as I live, his influence will mean more to me than that of any other people next to my father and mother."*

Tombstone Reunion

In 1941, Reverend Endicott Peabody returned to Tombstone to celebrate the 59th anniversary of his Southern Arizona ministry to the *"mining magnates, government officials, ore-handlers, teamsters, saloonkeepers and gamblers".* One of those "government officials" that Cotty spoke of with particular admiration and respect during his last visit to Tombstone had been a lawman and a gambler during the wild days of 1881-82. His name was Wyatt Earp. He and Cotty had been close back then and their friendship had lasted until Wyatt's death in Los Angeles in 1929 at the age of 80.

Wyatt Earp: 1923

A Targeted Killing

Lt. Howard B. Cushing

How Cushing Street Got Its Name

In 1942, Eve Ball, author and friend to many Mescalero Apaches (NM), convinced Asa (Ace) Daklugie, a Chiricahua Apache, to tell her the stories of his people's war with the United States of America and the Republic of Mexico (primarily 1861-1886).

These stories had been told many times by White-Eyes: historians, military officers, and ordinary pioneers who had the misfortune to encounter Apaches prior to Geronimo's surrender in 1886. This would be the first time these stories from the Apaches' perspective would be written down and published. It should come as no surprise that Daklugie's and other Apaches' accounts vary considerably from scholarly tomes, official (and largely self-serving) military reports, and hysterical newspaper accounts.

Asa Daklugie, who died in 1955, was the son of a Nednhi Chiricahua Apache chief named Juh. His name is a Spanish corruption of an Apache name that means "he sees ahead". It is pronounced Hó. In 1871, the Americans had never heard of Juh, mostly because the ancestral homeland of the Nednhi was the high, incredibly rugged Sierra Madre in Northern Mexico.

By contrast, in 1871 just about every American knew the name "Cochise", whose Chokonen Chiricahua Apache ancestral homeland was the Chiricahua and Dragoon Mountains of Southern Arizona. And it was upon Cochise's shoulders that the Americans placed the blame for almost all Apache depredations ... even when Cochise and his band were hundreds of miles distant at the time.

Lt. Cushing

In 1871, the Army's premier Indian fighter in Arizona Territory was 33-year-old Lt. Howard Cushing. He was courageous, smart, and cocksure of his military abilities. He was also relentless in pursuit of hostile Apaches. He took pride in knowing that he had killed more Apaches, mostly Mescaleros and Pinals (not to mention many Apache women and children), than any other U.S. Army officer.

Years later, John G. Bourke, once aid to General George Crook, remembered Cushing as energetic, cool & determined ... and "The bravest man I ever saw. He had made his name famous all over the southwestern border."

At one point, Cushing led an attack on a village of peaceful Mescalero Apaches in New Mexico. His soldiers left all the Indians dead except for two women, both of whom had been shot in the leg. Soon, other Mescaleros discovered the massacre and started to bury their dead. As they did, Cushing's troops stole their horses. Other Apache bands took notice, as we shall see.

Objective: Find & Crush Cochise

The U.S. Army was under great pressure by civilians in the Arizona & New Mexico Territories to wipe out any Apaches not on their respective reservation. The Army knew that to do this they had to capture or kill Cochise. Lt. Cushing became obsessed with finding, engaging, and destroying

The Whetstone Mountains. Little has changed since
Lt. Cushing fought the Apaches there in May 1871

Cochise and his band of renegades. He could easily imagine the advancement in rank & glory that would come from such a monumental achievement.

On April 26, 1871, Lt. Cushing and his column of seasoned troops set off from Fort Lowell (7 miles east of downtown Tucson) to track down and crush Cochise. Five days out, near Camp Crittenton (formerly Fort Buchanan) on Sonoita Creek, they saw burning grass in the distance. Cushing assumed that some of Cochise's band were signaling their relatives camped in the Whetstone Mountains. Knowing that the Indians were doing the burning, Cushing led his soldiers northeasterly in their direction.

Everywhere Cushing's troops rode, the grass was either burnt to the ground or still on fire. As they crossed the scorched earth, the Army horses started to wear out for lack of water and grass to eat. It did not seem to occur to Cushing to ask himself why the Indians are burning miles and miles of grassland.

Two miles north of the Bobocomari River, Sargeant John Mott discovered the tracks of a lone Apache woman and her pony. Cushing ordered Mott and two privates to go ahead of the main body of soldiers and follow her trail that seemed to be leading to Bear Springs in the Whetstone Mountains. Cushing's 20 soldiers would not be far behind the advance scouts.

We know from Mott's report that he thought something was odd. This Apache woman was making no effort to cover her trail. Apaches are notorious for being extremely difficult to track. But when this woman could have easily walked on rocks, she instead left her footprints in the dirt or sand. They led up into a steep canyon. Mott and his soldiers followed warily.

Trapped

Now Mott was beginning to put the pieces together. First the burning grass. Then the easily followed trail that led to a canyon well-suited for ambush. Suddenly, Mott veered off the trail and led his two privates up one side of the canyon. Too late.

The trap door slammed shut. From a hidden arroyo behind them sprang some 15 heavily armed Apaches. The soldiers turned and started to run the other way. Ahead of them, even more Apaches blocked their escape. The Indians opened fire killing one soldier's horse and seriously wounding one of the privates.

Mott and his 2 men returned fire, but they were helpless to warn Cushing, whom they knew would now be galloping to their rescue only to be similarly trapped. Mott, thinking the 3 had no chance to survive, suddenly realized that the Apaches were toying with them. One warrior rode up to the able-bodied private and snatched his hat from his head. A virtuoso performance of horsemanship and bravery.

Counting coup was characteristic of the Plains Indians; not Apaches. Unlike the Plains Indians, if they could help it, the Apaches never engaged in battle with the Mexican or American armies in the open. Apaches, however, were highly effective ambush killers. In their day, in Arizona, New Mexico, Sonora & Chihuahua, Apaches were the Alpha predators. But while exceedingly brave, they didn't risk the lives of their very limited number of warriors needlessly.

Lt. Cushing To The Rescue

Mott didn't have time to contemplate this strange behavior. He and his 2 men were still sitting ducks; and now Cushing and all of his 20 soldiers were storming up the canyon. Mott signaled to Cushing to go back, but Cushing was sure he had Cochise right where he wanted him.

The Indians opened fire once more. Immediately, 3 army horses fell. Then the lieutenant right next to Cushing was shot in the face; the bullet and brains exiting from the back of his head.

Now the Apaches charged. Many years later, Mott wrote, *"It seemed as if every rock and bush became an Indian."*

Mott turned to address the onslaught when he heard Cushing cry out. *"Sergeant, I am killed. Take me out. Take me out."* Mott saw his lieutenant fall on his face. He and another soldier tried desperately to get their commanding officer to safety. They had gone but 10 or 12 paces when an Apache sharpshooter sent a bullet crashing through Cushing face, killing him instantly.

Note: With bow and arrows, most Apache warriors were proficient hunters of large mammals, including humans. With the best Winchester repeating rifles, most were deadly accurate sharpshooters, well known among both Americans & Mexicans for head-shots, which almost always resulted in instant death.

Mott and the other soldier dropped Cushing's lifeless body and *"turned to sell our lives as dearly as possible."* They struggled down the canyon firing back at the attacking Apaches. Then, as suddenly as it had started, the fight was over. Clearly the Indians could have killed and seriously wounded many if not all of the surviving soldiers. Yet they let the soldiers escape. It was as if the Apaches had accomplished their goal. In the annals of the Apache Wars, nothing like this was ever reported.

To quote David Roberts, author of Once They Moved Like The Wind:

"Walking and riding through the night, abandoning exhausted pack mules, Mott's men staggered westward to Camp Critten-ton (present-day Sonoita). Besides the lieutenant, the patrol had lost only two men, with a third severely wounded. But the army's finest Apache fighter had been coaxed into a trap, then slain with selective precision. The war in Arizona and New Mexico would continue for another fifteen years, but the Apaches would never again kill an officer of equal rank."

Cochise Prevailed. Or Had He?

Cochise had once again prevailed. Or had he? For 90 years after this battle, historians assumed that Cochise had led the attack on Cushing. In the early 1960's, historian Dan Thrapp, doing research for an upcoming book, discovered Mott's "lost" report in the National Archives. In it, he described the Apache who led the attack.

"The Indians were well handled by their chief, a thick, heavy set man, who never dismounted from a small brown horse during the fight. They were not noisy or boisterous as Indians generally are, but paid great attention to their chief, whose designs I could guess as he delivered his instructions by gestures."

Juh

Immediately, Thrapp knew the Apache leader who had targeted Cushing could not have been Cochise. No one who ever saw Cochise would have described him as "thick, heavy set".

Thrapp, author of the Conquest of Apacheria, thought that the architect of the trap might have been Chief Juh. Thrapp knew from Juh's best friend and brother-in-law, Geronimo, that Juh stuttered. When he got excited he could not speak clearly, so Geronimo spoke for him. Without Geronimo by his side, Juh directed his warriors in battle with gestures.

This speculation was confirmed in 1980 with the publication of Eve Ball's *Indeh: An Apache Odyssey*. Juh's son, Asa Daklugie, told the backstory no White-Eyes knew. Many years earlier, he told Eve that his father had developed a personal obsession with Cushing, just as Cushing obsessed over Cochise. Juh had on many occasions sent scouts to spy on Cushing and report back the lieutenant's strategies and tactics; his strengths and weaknesses. On occasion, Juh and his warriors engaged in skirmishes with Cushing and his troops to learn more about his target and develop a strategy to trap him. At this time, neither Cushing nor anyone else in the U.S. Army had ever heard of Juh.

Said Juh's son, *"Other White-Eyes were killed too; I don't know how many. We weren't all the time counting the dead as soldiers did. Juh wasn't much interested in the troops ... just Cushing."*

In death, Lieutenant Howard Cushing became *"The Custer of Arizona".* In memorial, grateful Tucsonans named a street in his honor. Cushing Street is just south of the Tucson Convention Center. Today, the most important place on Cushing Street is the Cushing Street Bar & Restaurant, one of our favorites. They offer live jazz on Fri-

Lt. Cushing was originally buried at Ft. Lowell, but his remains were transferred to the cemetery at the San Francisco Presidio.

day and Saturday nights.

Our Tucson pioneer civic leaders honored a brave soldier. Such were the times however, they could never have recognized Cushing's racial bigotry, needless brutality, arrogance, and willful ignorance of Apache ways that jeopardized his soldiers' lives and led to his targeted death. Cushing fell for one of the oldest tricks in the Apache playbook ... executed flawlessly by a brilliant tactician no White-Eyes had ever heard of.

For his role in the Battle of Bear Springs, Sgt. Mott received the Congressional Metal of Honor.

****

Note: the 2 primary sources for this article were Once They Moved Like The Wind by David Roberts and Indeh: An Apache Odyssey by Eve Ball. You can find other references to Cushing and this battle on the Internet, but I found them questionable or inaccurate. Wikipedia's account is particularly flawed. James L. Haley's Apache: A History and Cultural Portrait refers to Juh as "a fat monster". I have read too much about Apaches of that era to agree. True, Juh was heavyset by Apache standards. To call him a "monster" is way too jingoistic. To Anglo and Mexican-Americans, he was no more vicious than Cochise, Victorio, Nana, Chihuahua, or Geronimo, who by the way were utterly vicious when on the warpath. But Juh was a great leader of his people, the Nednhi band of Chiricahua Apaches whose homeland was the Sierra Madre of Northern Mexico. jg

Apache May

An Indian Girl On The Slaughter Ranch

"Texas" John Slaughter was the sheriff who cleaned up Cochise County after the Earp Brothers and Doc Holliday left Arizona. He was as tough as they come and, among the outlaw class, earned the moniker "that wicked little gringo".

John Slaughter

As despised and feared as he was by the outlaws, he was highly respected and much appreciated by the law-abiding ranchers, merchants, and miners.

In 1896, ten years after Geronimo's final surrender, some disgruntled Apaches left the San Carlos Reservation and returned to a nomadic life of raiding both American and Mexican ranches.

The Apaches Attack And Kill
A Little Girl And Her Father

"While traveling by team and wagon from Pima, Arizona to Clifton, Arizona [Horatio Merril, age 58 and his daughter Eliza, age 4] were ambushed and killed by Indians with rifles December 3, 1895, shortly after sundown." So reads a roadside marker on State Route 70 east of Safford.

Eliza was wearing a distinctive white dress, or basque, tight at the waist, shaped by darts and many buttons down the front. The Apaches took the dress and other Merril possessions, including a fringed brown wool shawl.

A few years after the Merril murders, rancher Alfred Hand

was slaughtered by Apaches who stole whatever they could carry from his cabin near Cave Creek in the San Simon Valley, including a cloth Cochise County election poster made of white muslin with the names of Republican candidates in the election of 1888.

The Slaughter Ranch and Renegade Apaches

John Slaughter had one of the largest cattle operations in Arizona Territory at his San Bernardino Ranch 45 miles east of Bisbee on the International Border. Most of the Slaughter Ranch was in Mexico. He was used to Mexican outlaws trying to steal his cattle and most paid for their misdeeds with their lives. But Apaches stealing Mr. Slaughter's cattle was another matter, and the former Sheriff would need the assistance of the U.S. Army.

In early May, 1896, ranch foreman, Jesse Fisher, notified his boss that Apaches were camped in the Guadalupe Mountains south of the border. Horse soldiers, Army scouts, and ranch hands, perhaps 40 men in all, discovered the Apache's camp, but it was deserted. Scouts tracked the small Apache band to a new camp about 20 miles away. They attempted to sneak up on the Indians under cover of darkness, but were discovered. Some shots were fired, but the Apaches knew they were badly outnumbered. As was their practice, they just disappeared into the wilderness where the White Eyes couldn't follow.

When the soldiers and ranchers entered the Apache's camp, they found supplies of meat, corn, and mesquite beans. They also found stashes of plunder stolen from Americans and Mexicans: hatchets, scissors, needles and thread, black powder and reloading equipment and more. Here too they found a few Indian ponies, and 9 horses, four of which belonged to Mr. Slaughter.

In one of the wickiups, John Slaughter found an infant, a

girl perhaps a year old. He wrapped her in a brown, wool shawl he found nearby and took her back to his ranch.

It was not long before they realized that the child's shirt had been constructed from the dress of Eliza Merril. The brown shawl had also been Eliza's.

Moreover, the infant's dress was made from the cloth election poster the Apache's had stolen after they murdered Mr. Hand.

Apache May
Photo by C.S. Fly

John and his wife, Viola, named the child Apache May ... "May" for the month in which they found her. Another young foster child on the ranch named Lola started calling her 'Pache, which quickly became "Patchy".

Viola dressed "Patchy" in bright colored dresses, kept her reasonably clean and groomed, and began teaching her the ways of a successful 19th century American rancher, including table manners.

Attitudes Toward Apaches

It is not unheard of for 19th century hunters to kill wolves or other predators, and take home one or two of their orphans to see if they could domesticate them. A lot of people in Southeastern Arizona simply assumed that the Slaughters had done something similar.

To Mexican and American ranchers, miners, and merchants, the Apaches were vermin, albeit the most dangerous kind. They were a species not to be trifled with. Rather they were to be held in concentration camps known as reservations or eradicated. When we understand such attitudes, we can more easily see why Apache May became a minor celebrity in and around Tombstone and Bisbee.

Would this prosperous and prominent Cochise County family be able to domesticate a wild Indian? Or would Apache May revert to the villainous and amoral wild state of her people. In other words, "You can take an Indian out of the wild, but you can't take the wild out of an Indian." Such were the prevailing attitudes.

It was in this world that young Apache May became a "media star". The Slaughters took the girl to Tombstone on numerous occasions so the people could see her. The now-famous Old West photographer, C. S. Fly, took pictures of her that were then circulated to the newspapers.

Apache May Story In Tombstone Epitaph

On June 17, 1896, the Tombstone Epitaph published a lengthy story about the Slaughters and their young Apache.

"Mrs. J.H. Slaughter and her charming daughter, Miss Addie arrived in town today with the little Apache papoose from the San Bernardino Ranch."

"As soon as it became known that the papoose was in town, a steady stream of people visited Fly's Gallery to catch a glimpse of the young captive."

"Isn't she cute," said each of the ladies in their turn as the youngster sat mutely but calmly, munching on some cake."

"Her features were covered with a most propitious smile and she seemed tickled to death, which in turn, was contagious to the ladies present."

"The papoose is a chubby girl of about two or three years of age, with a good head of coarse, black hair, huge beautiful eyes, and for her size, is strong and healthy, and a com-

plexion color which distinguishes an Apache. The little papoose in her neat, red dress, clean face and parted hair makes her look indeed "cute"!"

"Mrs. Slaughter, who has inquired into the matter, and finding its mother has not returned to the reservation, has decided to adopt and raise the papoose. The entire family has become quite attached to the young captive, and if she takes kindly to civilized life will no doubt receive a liberal education, and be brought up in the way it should go. Mrs. Slaughter states 'Apache' as she has already been christened, takes kindly to her surroundings, and has become the pet of the San Bernardino Ranch."

Viola Slaughter with Apache May

Apache May and Don Juan

Of all the people at the ranch who doted on Apache May, it was clear to all that her favorite was John Slaughter. The attachment was mutual. She called him Don Juan and followed him around the ranch whenever she could. When he was gone from the ranch, 'Patchy' would sit on the porch for hours awaiting his return. She was happiest when she was riding on horseback with Don Juan.

On a cold February morning in 1900, some of the ranch children, including Patchy, were playing around a fire that had been started in the yard to boil water. Suddenly, Patchy's dress caught on fire. The terrified youngster ran away from the ranch house. Willie Slaughter, adult son of John by a previous marriage, heard her screams, and ran after the girl. But by the time Willie was able to smother the flames, Patchy had severe burns over much of her little body.

The Slaughter ranch house and out-buildings are about 18 miles east of the City of Douglas. But in 1900, Douglas didn't exist. The closest doctor was in Bisbee, 45 miles away. Fortunately, the ranch had a telephone line to Bisbee and Dr. Dudley was called immediately.

He gave first aid instructions over the telephone, then headed for the ranch. But in his horse and buggy, it took him over 8 hours before he could personally attend to the little girl.

Patchy suffered horribly. At one point she told Mr. Slaughter, *"Don Juan, I'm going to die."* When Dr. Dudley arrived, he assessed the situation. By then the girl was in shock and her vital signs were very weak.

He told John and Viola that there was no hope. Apache May died the next morning. The Slaughters were devastated.

Jesse, the ranch foreman, fashioned a small coffin of rough lumber and lined it with cloth. She was buried in the ranch cemetery.

Today, you can visit "Texas" John Slaughter's San Bernardino Ranch and we recommend you do. It is a fitting museum to the man and his family who did so much to civilize Southeastern Arizona. You can read Roger Naylor's story "Texas" John Slaughter: Arizona's Meanest Little Good Guy, on page 53 of this book.

Tale of the Devil Dog

Some of our SouthernArizonaGuide.com readers have asked about the image of a dog in our Southern Arizona Guide banner and the words: Devil Dog Productions LLC. That's our dog, Buddy. And Devil Dog is our production company. It consists of Ms. Karen, myself (Jim), two MacBook-Pros, two Canon Rebels and 6 lenses, an IPhone, a Samsung Android S5, and Bud. He goes by "Bud" or "Buddy" in the same way Superman goes by Clark Kent.

Bud is a very important member of our team. I'll explain. Years ago, when we first moved to Tucson from L.A., Ms. Karen planted a substantial rose garden just beyond the kitchen window. She also planted many other kinds of plants out and about and so our yard has beautiful flowers nearly everywhere. But in the beginning, there was this little problem: rabbits.

Rabbits would get in the yard and make delicious salads out of Ms. Karen's roses and other plants. We spent a lot of time just chasing them out. One hot July afternoon, we walked out on the main patio and saw 13 rabbits all stretched out on the grass in the shade casually munching away. Now I could empathize with Elmer Fudd and my affinity for Bugs Bunny was waning fast. Something had to be done, but what?

I matter-of-factly explained to Ms. Karen that I could shoot them. "You can't shoot bunnies," she exclaimed in horror. "They're so cute."

"Well, what then," I asked.

"We'll get a dog," she said. And that was the end of that discussion. Off we went to the dog pound on Silverbell Road.

The Prison

The Animal Care Shelter is a very unpleasant place, despite the heroic efforts of some of the staff and volunteers. The animals are all in cages - two or three to a cage. Cold concrete floors. Urine and feces. The smell would gag a vulture.

We had been there about an hour and looked at perhaps 60 or more dog possibilities. None seemed just right and we were discouraged. As we were about to leave I spotted one we must have overlooked. He had a yellow-blonde coat. He was thin. His eyes were sad, as if he had seen so many people pass his cage without giving him consideration that he had given up all hope of ever getting out of this awful prison.

But there was something about this particular dog that seemed special. The eyes, perhaps. We looked at his papers. Lab-Mix. Been there for more than 2 months. I motioned for the guard to put a leash on him so we could take him outside, walk around a little, and get to know each other.

The Animal Care people have a small fenced dirt area out back where you can take a dog, sit on a bench, and get acquainted. We chatted with this scrawny, dirty dog for a few minutes. He was friendly enough, but not desperately needy. He had a certain dignity that you don't see in many canines. He was a prisoner, but he hadn't been broken. His spirit was still strong.

The Great Beast, a few days after his first bath and decent meal since being released from prison.

The Contract

I told Ms. Karen that I think this is the one. She seemed skeptical. I said, "Let me handle the negotiations." I got Dog's attention. "Here's the deal," I said. "We're offering two square meals a day, an occasional bone, a big yard, and a clean place to sleep. All you have to do is keep the rabbits out of our gardens. What do you say?"

Dog looked at me in disbelief. "You mean you're going to get me outa this dump and feed me decent meals, and all I have to do is chase rabbits?"

"Bunnies," Ms. Karen corrected. "They're bunnies and we don't want you to kill them or eat them or anything like that. Just keep them out of my gardens."

"Deal," said Dog. And he signed the contract right then and there. We took him home, gave him a much needed bath, and fed him the first decent food he'd had in months. We named him Buddy. He didn't seem to mind.

More Than We Bargained For

Several weeks passed and Buddy upheld his part of the bargain. Rabbit - I mean bunny - problem solved. But as time passed, we began to suspect that there was something different about this dog. We thought we had acquired a pure bred mutt. But the regal way he carried himself, tail aloft as if a flag of defiance. His native intelligence and keen hunting instinct. That black mark on this tongue. Surely the sign of The Devil.

And finally, his howl; wild, primitive, sorrowful. When coyotes in the distance begin to howl in concert at night, Bud joins in the chorus, much to the appreciation of our neighbors, I'm sure. It's a beautiful thing to hear at 2 AM.

All characteristic of that rarest and most magnificent breed: **Genuine Sonoran Devil Dog**. So rare, the AKA doesn't even have one registered.

The Rattlesnake

It wasn't long before we were certain of our good fortune. One day Ms. Karen was working in her garden and Bud started to bark at something in the bushes a few feet away. But this wasn't his usual bark. Bud despises coyotes (except when they're singing in the distance). When they come up around the fence line, he gives them his most ferocious bark-growl-bark. The hair on his back stands straight up. We had become accustomed to the sound. It's deep and full - the kind that strikes terror in little bunnies. In BunnyLand he's known as **The Great Beast.**

But now he was barking at something in the bushes and the sound was high-pitched, easily distinguishable from his regular coyote bark. We went to investigate. Sure enough, a five-foot diamondback, coiled and ready to strike at Ms. Karen.

We've heard that snake-bark many times since. Sometimes it's just Elmo, our resident gopher snake who looks almost exactly like a rattler. Usually, it's a rattler. The Devil Dog keeps Ms. Karen's gardens safe from bunnies and us humans safe from rattlesnakes. For that, we have honored Bud by naming our little company after him. He doesn't seem to mind.

Resources

The following are a few of the reference books used to develop the stories in this anthology. We believe them to be among the most authoritative. Some historical journals were also used. The Internet has many articles on these subjects. However, care must be taken because many websites, particularly Wikipedia, are rife with historical inaccuracies.

Apache

Al Sieber: Chief of Scouts. Thrapp, Dan L., Worcester, Donald E. University of Oklahoma Press.

Apaches: A History and Culture Portrait. Haley, James L. University of Oklahoma Press

Apache Voices: Their Stories of Survival as Told to Eve Ball. Robinson, Sherry. University of New Mexico Press.

Big Sycamore Stands Alone: The Western Apaches, Aravaipa, and the Struggle for Place. Record, Ian W. University of Oklahoma Press.

Cochise: Firsthand Accounts of the Chiricahua Apache Chief. Editor: Sweeney, Edwin R. University of Oklahoma Press.

The Conquest of Apacheria. Thrapp, Dan L. University of Oklahoma Press.

From Cochise to Geronimo: The Chiricahua Apaches, 1874 to 1886. Sweeney, Edwin R. University of Oklahoma Press.

Indeh: An Apache Odyssey, with New Maps Paperback. Eve Ball. University of Oklahoma Press.

Civil War in Apacheland: Sergeant George Hand's Diary, 1861-1864. Hand, George. Editor: Carmony, Neil B. High Lonesome Books.

Once They Moved Like The Wind : Cochise, Geronimo, And The Apache Wars. Roberts, David. A Touchstone Book (Simon & Schuster).

Gatewood and Geronimo. Kraft, Louis. University of New Mexico Press.

Geronimo: His Own Story: The Autobiography of a Great Patriot Warrior. Geronimo. Editor: Barrett, S. M. Plume.

In the Days of Victorio; Recollections of a Warm Springs Apache. Eve Ball, James Kaywaykla. University of Arizona Press.

Tombstone

A Tenderfoot in Tombstone, the Private Journal of George Whitwell Parsons: The Turbulent Years, 1880-82. George W. Parsons. Editor: Lynn R. Bailey. Western Lore Press.

Doc Holliday: The Life and Legend. Roberts, Gary L. John Wiley & Sons.

The Last Gunfight: The Real Story of the Shootout at the O.K. Corral And How It Changed the American West. Guinn, Jeff. Simon & Schuster.

Wyatt Earp: The Life Behind the Legend. Casey Tefertiller. John Wiley & Sons.

Tucson

Tucson: The Life and Times of an American City. Sonnichsen, C. L. University of Oklahoma Press.

Whiskey, Six-Guns and Red-Light Ladies: George Hand's Saloon Diary, Tucson, 1875-1878. Hand, George. Editor: Carmony, Neil B.

Yesterday's Tucson Today: Your Guide to Walking the Historic Towns of the Santa Cruz Valley. Cuming, Harry. West Press.

General – Southern Arizona

The Great Arizona Orphan Abduction Gordon, Linda. Harvard University Press.